In 2004, I was given a reminder of the devastating cost of suffering in silence. Some of our team at Auto Trader went out after work to watch an England football match in the European Championships. Our boss had kindly put some money behind the bar and I remember us all cheering England to a rare victory at that time. What nobody noticed that evening was the young lad who decided to go home at half-time.

We never saw Ben again because he killed himself that night. A young man for whom life was no longer bearable. His closest colleagues were beside themselves and incredibly shocked. He had been laughing and joking in the office only 24 hours earlier. How much must Ben have been suffering in silence? He was surrounded by so many people, yet he must have felt so alone. My passionate pledge to myself is to no longer hide my anxiety and to do everything I can to reduce the ignorance and stigma that surrounds mental health.

If you're suffering, please don't wait any longer to break your silence. The longer you hold on to things, the heavier they become and the harder it is not to feel as desperate as poor Ben.

This book is for you if...

You lead an organisation or business

Leaders play a pivotal role in shaping their organisation's culture and environment. We need to invest in human sustainability; this book will help leaders do that. Creating kinder cultures is critical to sustainable growth. This book is for leaders who want to cultivate environments that prioritise mental wellbeing and foster healthier, more productive teams.

You work for an organisation or business

Navigating the complexities of work today while looking after your mental health can be very challenging. This book provides practical insights and strategies to help people manage stress, strengthen resilience and cultivate a positive mindset. Whether facing workplace pressures, interpersonal conflicts, or personal challenges, it gives actionable guidance to help support mental health in the workplace.

You care about your mental health

Mental health transcends age, gender, ethnicity and occupation. This book is for anyone who recognises the importance of prioritising their mental wellbeing. It will give you some of the tools you need to build emotional resilience, take better care of yourself and navigate the inevitable ups and downs of life.

You want to support others who are struggling

Supporting someone through mental health challenges requires empathy, understanding and knowledge.

It can be difficult to know how to do this well. Whether you're a family member, friend, colleague or manager, this book will give you the insights and strategies to offer meaningful support to those struggling with mental health issues. In addition to providing insights, this book provides practical, actionable advice to enable you to provide help and support.

'What's the bravest thing you've
ever said?' asked the boy.
'Help,' said the horse.'

'The Boy, the Mole,
the Fox and the Horse'
Charlie Mackesy

What people are saying...

'I've known David personally and professionally for many years. He is incredible and his work helping people to break their silence is truly inspirational. I know how proud he is to publish this book and I'm hugely confident it will make a massive difference to so many people. Outside of his day job, he is my daughter's godfather. Need I say more?'
Sharon Slattery, ex-UK Sales Director of Auto Trader

'I invited David into Wave within six weeks of opening our business. It was important for me to create a culture of kindness from day one and there was no better way of doing this than by inviting David to talk to our employees. He was instrumental in helping us break down the stigma of discussing mental health. Every organisation needs a David Beeney.'
Jane Austin, Director of HR at Wave Utilities

'When you first meet David, his warmth and authenticity strike you the most. This really helps people relate to him and confide in him. Fossil has supported his mission to break the silence for many years. I've never encountered anyone as passionate about helping people with their mental health as David is.'
Sarah Dunn, HR Director Europe North at Fossil Group, Inc.

'David's authenticity and passion shine through in his delivery. These qualities enable him to connect and engage employees across all areas of our business on the importance of focusing on their wellbeing. David has a genuine interest and commitment to understanding our culture so that employees can break their silence without fear.'
Ellen Bigmore, Head of HR at Safran Electrical & Power

'David's honesty about his journey and the tools he shared with us had a huge impact on our colleagues. It helped break the silence, opening up more opportunities for conversations about mental health with empathy and care.'
Siân Evans, Director of Leadership & Colleague Experience at Simplyhealth

'We are all human and have things going on outside of work, so in breaking the silence, we can create a kinder culture that builds deeper levels of trust, where people can truly thrive and be themselves. David's story and passion for building kinder cultures are truly inspiring. I cannot recommend his work highly enough. I will take him with me wherever I go!'
Nicki Burge, People Director at Direct Online Services

'Creating a kinder culture aligns perfectly with our values and everything we strive to achieve. David's work with us has enabled us to continue embedding our values and breaking the silence by encouraging more conversations about mental health.'
Corinne Spillane, Chief People Officer at Liaison Group

'David has been delivering wellbeing workshops for staff in our organisation for the past four years. The sessions have been so popular that many participants say they are the best workshops of their kind they have ever attended.'
Sarah Brewer, Head of Employee Experience at Public Health Wales

'We invited David to work with Yorkshire Housing to help us start a different type of conversation about mental health at work. David's ability to connect with and inspire everyone he meets is a rare talent. His authenticity, personal vulnerability and natural gift for storytelling have helped us break the silence around mental health and address many barriers to people opening up.'
Nina Evison, Executive Director of Culture & Performance at Yorkshire Housing

'Bringing mental health awareness support into our organisation wasn't something I did lightly. David broke the silence for us by bringing real-life experience and practical solutions to coping with them. He helped us talk openly and freely about how we were feeling and gave his time and ear to those who wanted to talk more.'
Claire Wishart, Head of HR at Calnex Solutions

'David talks from the heart, which is incredibly brave, and peppers his sessions with light-hearted anecdotes. This openness allowed our team to feel safe and secure, allowing them to share their vulnerabilities and create a stronger and more understanding environment.'
Emma Brierley, Director of Talent & Development at Broadwick Soho

'David's journey inspires those who have endured the weight of silence, encouraging individuals to embrace authenticity and be their true selves. In a world where mental health concerns are often swept under the carpet, this book and David's work guide people to building a workplace culture that prioritises the wellbeing of its people and breaks the silence.'
Julie Clarke, VP Global Employee Experience & Engagement at Sutherland

'David is inspirational and relentless in his drive to break the silence around mental wellbeing. He has spoken at many of our events and has had a far-reaching and long-lasting impact on thousands.'
Matt Manners, CEO & Founder of Inspiring Workplaces

'I've known David since the early 1990s when no one talked about mental health, especially in the workplace. When I saw his work change that, I asked him to come in to help my team and me at Vanarama. I saw first-hand that he was playing a huge role in not just changing that but making it unusual NOT to talk about it. I always thought he could write his book. I'm delighted he's finally helping even more people break their silence.'
Andy Alderson, Former CEO of Vanarama

'David approaches everything he does with infectious kindness and compassion. He is truly inspirational and a master at creating space to allow people to take a breath and focus on their mental health.'
Jo Purser, Head of Strategic HR & OD at NHS England

'Getting to know David has been such a valuable experience for me personally and professionally. David's journey is real and relatable and shows that taking that first step is scary, but brave, and demonstrates true strength. He has helped us remove 'mental health' as the elephant in the room.' In that way, David has truly helped us to break the silence.'
Letitia Winston, Senior Mental Wellbeing Specialist at Grundfos Pumps

'When it comes to mental wellbeing, David's compassionate approach, candid sharing of personal experiences, and skilful and humorous storytelling make him an exceptional and trusted partner for me and many others. He first broke his silence at Auto Trader and is now helping thousands of others to break their silence too.'
Dani Baldwin Rowe, Internal Communications Manager at Auto Trader

'The stories we tell about workplace wellbeing are an important part of how organisations will change for the better. By sharing his story so openly, David has helped employers break the silence about mental health. In doing so, he has played a key part in helping leaders understand how vulnerability helps them build kinder cultures.'
Gethin Nadin, Chief Innovation Officer at Benefex

'David has a genuine passion and positive energy in advocating for a kinder culture in the workplace and has helped us break the silence. If you can combine this with a high-performance culture, you have the foundations for a highly successful business.'
Paul Maberly, Managing Partner at Mercer & Hole

'The way David brings his vulnerability and authenticity to his workshops really helps to build trust. It inspires people to break their silence regarding mental health and instils kinder cultures within teams across all levels.'
Hiran Odedra, Head of Diversity, Equality & Inclusion at Mercedes Benz Grand Prix

'David's courageous honesty about his struggles is a powerful reminder of the importance of addressing mental health with the same gravity as physical health. His message that it's ok not to be ok gives hope to those who may be silently suffering and says that seeking support is a sign of strength.'
Emma Pickering, Director of People at ProMedical

'David has taught me life-changing skills to support and develop my mental wellbeing. The sessions he has delivered for all our employees have inspired many to break their silence. He will continue to make a massive difference to people's mental wellbeing and, in the process, save many lives.'
Barry Gavahan, Group CEO at DES Group

About David Beeney

David Beeney enjoyed a very successful 30-year career in the world of media. But, during that time, he was hiding something. Eventually in 2016, he found the courage to open up about the most significant struggle of his life: his mental health. A secret battle with panic attacks meant years of torment and angst. David's decision to break his silence was one of the most significant moments of his life. Today, David's business, Breaking The Silence, is regarded as one of the world's leading advisors on mental health in the workplace. He has worked with leading global brands including HSBC, McDonald's and Google.

In the UK, he has advised the likes of the NHS, the Labour Party, Sainsbury's, the Mercedes Formula One team and the Royal Navy. David is a qualified mental health counsellor and a registered member of the British Association of Counsellors and Practitioners (BACP). He has also been a trustee for Mind, the mental health charity. In 2024, he was once more recognised as one of the top global influencers in employee engagement by his peers.

This book is dedicated to all
those currently suffering in
silence with their mental health.
I wrote this book for you and for those around you
who can help you break your silence.

It's time for action

This book was launched during Mental Health Awareness Week in 2024. During that week, my message was clear: the time for awareness has long gone. It's now time for action and this book is part of my contribution to that action. Having read it, I hope it encourages you to act whether that be for yourself, your teams or your organisation.

My workshops, which typically involve group interaction, examples and practical exercises are always very popular with my clients. You have read some of the testimonials and feedback I've had from the people and organisations with whom I've worked over the years. I have consistently seen clear evidence that my sessions not only inspire employees to place greater emphasis on self-care but also drive energy throughout these businesses by creating kinder cultures.

In those sessions I share my personal story of suffering in silence and we also explore the causes, stigma and some of the myths around mental health. Practical steps such as implementing regular check-ins and using a framework for best practice mental health conversations are taken back into the workplace with much greater confidence and understanding and this creates an improved culture of openness and trust.

Many of my clients now regard these workshops as an essential module on their leadership development programmes and I believe these sessions should be mandatory for anybody with people management responsibility. Ideally the first session would be delivered to the senior leadership team. I have also delivered workshops for countless teams of Mental Health First Aiders and Wellbeing Champions, providing both their induction training and ongoing development sessions.

I also share my story of over 30 years of suffering in silence with much larger numbers at conferences, town-hall style meetings, and lunch and learn sessions. The content is tailored to every audience, but I always remind organisers that mental health issues can impact everybody within a business, regardless of seniority or status.

It's time to break the silence. To do so, action is now required and, as you'll read in the following pages, helping people to take that action is now my life's work. Please get in touch if I can help.

www.breakingthesilence.co.uk

ENABLING EMPLOYERS TO UNDERSTAND MENTAL HEALTH

David Beeney

Published by
Filament Publishing Ltd
14, Croydon Road, Beddington,
Croydon, Surrey CR0 4PA
+44(0)20 8688 2598
www.filamentpublishing.com

ISBN 978-1-915465-52-8
Printed in UK
Book layout by Ana Celia Silva

જ

Table of Contents

Introduction 10,849 days 16

1. If only it were perfect 19

2. The two days that changed my life 23

3. Your struggles can be super strengths 31

4. Breaking my silence 39

5. Can you measure your mental health? 45

6. 52 out of 60 53

7. One in one 59

8. Creating kinder cultures 67

9. Adults need playtime 75

10. Don't be a frog 81

11. A can of worms 87

12. Lower your bar 93

13. Notice, don't interpret 99

14. Inspiring others by sharing vulnerability 105

15. Put your oxygen mask on first 111

16. The proof of the pudding 117

17. The clock is ticking 121

A final thought 125

Thank you 129

Notes and further reading 137

Introduction
10,849 days

10,849 days. It's a long time. Long enough to build the Empire State Building and for humanity to plan and execute its first moon landing. Incredibly, it's also the exact amount of time that passed before I could talk about the day that would ultimately change my life. On 2 September 1986, I suffered a mental crisis at work and, as a result, aged 24 thought my career was over. 30 years later, or 10,849 days to be precise, I eventually broke my silence.

Why didn't I break my silence earlier? Why did I wait so long to talk about my experience of mental ill-health? And, by not doing so, did I waste all those years? Many people have asked me those questions and I've often asked myself the same. The truth is that, if I had, my work now would be much less powerful. I would have had less experience with the slings and arrows that life can throw at any of us. I would empathise less with those I now support because I wouldn't know what it's like to suffer in silence. I wouldn't have had the time to become a fully qualified mental health counsellor with all the credibility that brings to my work and the opportunity that affords me to help others. And, finally, observing countless teams and workplaces over that time, has led me to truly understand the commercial benefits of kinder cultures. I now think of those 30 years as a brilliant apprenticeship at the end of which I was able to discover my true purpose in life. Importantly, those 30 years of learning about the stigma which surrounds mental health in the workplace and the power unleashed by the creation of a culture of kindness meant I could make a difference quickly in the world of work once I had discovered my purpose.

This book is about that purpose, why that matters and what you can do to break the silence around mental health. I have now committed the rest of my working life to helping millions of others break their silence. Those people who are too scared to be honest about their mental health. Those who fear the consequences it may bring and those who struggle to find anyone with a listening ear. Employers have a huge role to play in eradicating the stigma of mental health. So many cultures do not make the time or space for those honest and open conversations vital to everyone's wellbeing. Those who do make time shine very brightly and, encouragingly, I'm seeing more employees than ever benefitting from the impact of the creation of kinder workplace cultures. Crucially, I'm also talking to more and more employers who are clear about the commercial benefit this brings.

I often hear people say that creating kinder cultures is a fluffy subject, only relevant to certain types of business. Those people could not be more wrong. It's a subject that should be fundamental to the vision and mission of any and every company. Only by prioritising and optimising wellbeing can people truly flourish in the workplace.

This idea is at the heart of my book and encompasses everything I've been sharing during the most rewarding years of my career. It's a book that will help you on your journey, whether you are an employer, employee or simply interested in helping yourself. For my part, it's a book that has given me even greater resolve and passion to walk the road that is still less travelled. We desperately need to reframe our view of mental health and build kinder cultures everywhere.

To do that, we need to break the silence.

'You are braver than you believe,
stronger than you seem,
and smarter than you think.'

A. A. Milne

Chapter 1
If only it were perfect

The working week ended with a brief team meeting. Everyone was brimming with confidence, energy and positivity. Sales were soaring, a new team member had settled in brilliantly and everyone's wellbeing scores were heading in the right direction. The team knew that because their business valued wellbeing scores ahead of revenue or profit numbers.

In this regular Friday get-together, chit-chat flowed and animated conversations always centred on everyone's feelings and what was happening in their lives. The team leader knew that creating structured time for these unstructured conversations was critical. Everyone in that team cared enough about each other to know the little details that mattered: pets' names, children's passions, personal hobbies and what fired people up when they left the office. The famous quote by Mark Twain - that the two most important days in your life are the day you are born and the day you work out why - was framed on a key visible wall of the office. Sitting on some of the desks were cans of baked beans. Most newcomers asked why the beans were there and almost always got the same answer.

'It's Beeney's way of encouraging us to be more open about our mental health. He says it's ok to spill your beans!'

Soon, the chat turned to issues affecting how people felt. One of the team members was going through a very tough time and as was usually the case, no one minded creating the space to discuss how that felt. Not everyone always wanted to discuss these things, and no one was ever under pressure to do so. But at least everyone was safe in the knowledge that these conversations were always seen as a sign of strength and not weakness. On this day, one of the team members talked about something that had been on their mind for a long time. It was personal and professional, and this person revealed their vulnerability at every turn. The fact that it was one of the line managers going through this made no difference to the conversation. It was the norm in the context of this company. There were no hierarchies when it came to wellbeing. The more senior the individual, the more open they were at work. The CEO had a favourite phrase about a fish rotting from its head and she always used it because she was honest about her mental health and the need to model the behaviour she wanted to see in the company culture.

Her colleagues' physical, psychological and emotional wellbeing were the things she cared about the most. She was famous for putting the wellbeing of her people at the heart of the business, even firing several clients when it became clear that their behaviour was having a detrimental effect on the people working on their business. Wellbeing was always the first line item to get additional investment in the business and it was the area of the company around which the board had the most comprehensive metrics. It was also the first discussion in any appraisal.

As always, that week's Friday afternoon get-together finished with everyone wishing each other a good weekend. As in most businesses, there had been many ups and downs that week, but the team all felt a massive commitment to each other. Here was a team that had each other's backs. They had all been trained on how important it was to spot the signs when someone was feeling off-colour mentally. And they all knew that their mental health mattered more than anything. From the CEO downwards, no one felt any stigma in raising this subject with anyone in the team.

Sound familiar? Sadly not. While some companies have made considerable strides in their approach to wellbeing, most haven't. They choose instead to focus on short-term profit and satisfying shareholder needs, even though there is now plenty of evidence that businesses with the best employee wellbeing are the most productive, creative and profitable. The picture of a world of work I painted just now is one we can only ever dream of. In fact, to my eternal sadness, it's a world we are unlikely to see even in my lifetime. And yet, more people than ever before are experiencing mental health problems in the workplace. We are in the middle of a mental health crisis dwarfed only by the scale of the problem of global warming. And, just like the climate crisis, people ignore what is quite patently staring at them. People in the workplace are less happy, less open, less fulfilled, less engaged and less mentally healthy than at any time in recent history. The stigma of mental health hangs over the workplace just as heavily as the 3,000 gigatons, and rising, of carbon dioxide which hangs over our planet. And just as that human-made smog is choking our wonderful planet, the stigma of mental health is choking everything that should be joyful about the world of work.

The unfolding mental health crisis is now all around us. To solve it, we must do one thing. And that is to eradicate the stigma of mental health in the workplace once and for all. The journey towards that goal is now my life's work and the only reason for writing this book. A book that will provide people with a roadmap to make a difference in the world and look after themselves and the people around them. In my most optimistic moments I believe that this book can also act as a rallying cry for a new movement dedicated to putting the wellbeing of every employee in the world at the heart of what companies do best and care about most. At the very least, it can shine a light on a subject close to my heart and one where I am desperate to see real change in my lifetime. For that change to happen, any lights that this book can ignite must be the catalyst for millions more lights illuminating the way to a world of work in which kinder cultures are the norm and the stigma of mental health is gone forever.

Our mental health crisis cannot be solved by world leaders, politicians or corporate giants that sit astride the world's financial markets. It will be solved by those like you and me who believe that people are our planet's most remarkable asset today. Giving individuals the tools they need to take care of their wellbeing and remove the stigma of mental health in the workplace is one of the most significant challenges of our age. And it's the focus of the pages to come.

It is time to start breaking the silence.

'There is no standard normal.
Normal is subjective.
There are seven billion versions
of normal on this planet.'

Matt Haig

Chapter 2
The two days that changed my life

Everyone has moments in their life that change everything forever. Those moments may be good or bad. They may be big or small, frightening or comforting. They often revolve around the circle of life: a child's birth or a parent's death. I've even met people whose lives have changed the first time they joined a choir or learned to paint. And in football, I've seen an FA Cup win rewrite a team's history. A feat that, sadly, my beloved Watford has yet to achieve. Whatever that moment, it changes people, whether for better or worse. And it can change the direction of their life forever too.

So it was for me on that September day I referred to earlier. I remember it well. It was a beautiful day – one of those days you sometimes get in early September which make you feel that summer hasn't quite ended. As I write this, I can still feel the heat coming through the windscreen as I drove to work that morning of the 2 September 1986. I was 24 years old and in a great place in my life: happy, fulfilled and secure. I had just been promoted and was enjoying both getting to grips with my new role as a sales trainer and all the things life was affording me. Confidence was not something I lacked so when my boss, Judy, told me we had someone coming in for an interview at 11 o'clock and asked if I would mind helping her with the interview, I couldn't wait to share the stage with her. Not only had I been entrusted with being a trainer to the sales team, but I was now considered senior enough to interview people! My suit may not have been very well cut, with a tendency to crease easily and in a particularly unflattering shade of brown, but I felt like a man at the top of his game. I confess that I've never been a style icon, much as I thought at the time that a brown suit was the height of sophistication. I suspect that description will make my family laugh though.

Flexing my brown suit, I strode into the interview room, thinking that I was seizing the moment whereas, in fact, this moment would take charge of me and change the course of my life. The memory of walking into that room, that moment of the calm before the storm, has remained with me and I can still recall every tiny detail. The room seemed so small that it was almost hobbit sized. And, straight away, I noticed how hot it was; the room felt sweltering, like an oven in the summer. And then there was the guy. The guy who had woken up that morning hoping that his career would change forever with this one interview only to be greeted by me, a man half his age, sweating profusely and dressed in a brown ill-fitting suit. The only saving grace was that he was sweating more than I was.

We stared at each other for what seemed like an eternity. What a classic sales archetype this man was. He would not have looked out of place with a set of encyclopaedias under his arm in the old days, trying to sell his wares to any unsuspecting passer-by. Working in sales was his life and he would do it until his dying day. I had no idea what he really thought of me, but imposter syndrome had taken hold in my head. Why it happened in that moment I will never know but suddenly I could hear him asking himself why he had to be interviewed by a man only half his age who clearly had no idea what he was doing. His face said it all: apathy, disdain and a dollop of contempt all rolled into one. However, despite the temperature in the room, which seemed to be increasing by the minute and the gnawing sense of anxiety at the back of my mind, I still felt excited to be interviewing someone for the first time.

Judy did everything you'd expect from a consummate sales professional. She was eloquent and articulate and spoke passionately and engagingly about the business, its mission and its future. In her capable hands, our interviewee smiled, laughed and nodded excitedly. I was enjoying the way Judy presented our business until she stopped suddenly and asked me a question.

'David, could you now just run through the company's induction programme please?'

This was my moment; I knew the induction programme inside out and this was where I got to show that I wasn't just a boy in a brown suit but a talented professional. But it didn't happen. The spotlight was on me but all I could feel was the heat and that awful sense of increasing anxiety, something I had never really experienced before. I must have stared blankly back at her because she had to ask a second time. Flushing with embarrassment, I nervously shuffled in my chair, muttering an almost inaudible 'yes'. And then, quite suddenly, I could feel it happening, although I had no idea what 'it' was at this stage of my young life. It hit me like a ten-ton truck: going from looking forward to the interview to suddenly feeling overwhelmed with anxiety. My chest tightened and breathing became difficult. My heart was pounding and racing in my ribcage while my head felt so tight that I thought it might explode. And, almost worst of all, that rising, uncontrollable wave of panic and fear washing up over me – something I had never experienced before. As I started to speak, I could feel all these things happening at once.

The confident David Beeney that had walked tall into the office that morning had been reduced within a few seconds to a gibbering wreck. Not at the hand of a person or by a specific event but because of something I couldn't explain. The more I tried to speak, the shakier my voice became. I was also acutely aware that I was struggling with my breathing. 'What would happen if my breathing became so bad that I couldn't speak?' said the demon voice inside my pounding head. Adrenaline was pumping through my veins at what felt like a hundred miles an hour and I suddenly found myself completely unable to speak and on the verge of vomiting. My chest was now so tight that I was beginning to panic that I wouldn't be able to breathe.

Try as I might, I just couldn't say anything; I was like a baby trying to get my first words out. Time stopped, but the banging in my head didn't. I was terrified. What was happening? Why was I so hot and sweating uncontrollably? Was it the heat in the room? Should I feign illness and pretend to collapse to avoid the embarrassment of what my boss and a stranger had just witnessed? Or was I really sick? As all these questions rushed through my head, I could feel two pairs of eyes bearing down on me, one pair puzzled, the other slightly worried. Judy looked concerned.

'Are you ok, David?'

'No, I'm not. I'm so sorry.' I replied with difficulty as I buried my head in my hands. At that moment, if the earth had opened and swallowed me, I wouldn't have minded. At least in that scenario, the excruciating buzzing and pounding in my head would have stopped.

'Well... ok. Let me just finish the interview. You go and wait for me in that room over there,' Judy said with the empathy you'd expect from a woman with a kind heart and an instinct for wellbeing. I remember walking out of that room utterly bemused, exhausted and mortified. I had no idea what had happened but I was aware that I was starting to feel calmer. Perhaps it was the sense of claustrophobia created by that tiny room and the pounding in my head. Perhaps it just wasn't my day. But I couldn't help feeling terrible that I'd let myself and my boss as well as the company down. This interview had been my big moment to shine and I'd been overcome by something I still couldn't explain. After waiting for what felt like an eternity, Judy suddenly appeared with a massive smile. She could see that I was feeling better.

'David, thank goodness you're ok. Forget about whatever happened in there today. These things happen so don't worry about it. The good news is that we've got another interview tomorrow at the same time. Ample opportunity for you to get your interview boots back on.'

And with that, she left. Neither Judy nor I spoke about it for the rest of that day, but it wasn't long before the demons started to return. As the day wore on, I could only think about 11 o'clock the next day. Would it happen again? In those days, I still lived with my parents. And yet, mentioning my day to them didn't occur to me. Nor did it occur to me to tell anyone else about it either. As I think about that now, I can barely believe that I didn't talk to anyone about what had happened. I created a wall of silence around one of the most frightening things that I had ever experienced. But then I think about the walls of silence that still exist in so many organisations today and

I forgive myself for not speaking sooner about what happened in that small, sweaty room on that fateful September day.

Inevitably, the next day arrived. But not until after I had to endure the only night of my life without sleep. Uncertainty mixed with anxiety was a potent cocktail for my brain which was still trying to come to terms with the day's events. I now realise that the day that followed was the first day I wore my mask. The mask that I was to wear for decades. The cacophony of noise inside my head and my pounding heart had been a panic attack and, despite my best efforts, it happened again. But this time it was different. It was a different day and another person: a young woman with a generous smile who could not have done more to put me at ease. As if it needed to be that way round but I suspect she could detect what she thought was nervousness. If only she had known that it was several stages beyond that. For a moment, because she was so different to the previous interviewee, I felt a glimmer of hope that the previous day may have been a one-off and this time would be better.

I could not have been more wrong. It felt like Groundhog Day. I was sitting in the same chair, wearing the same suit and it was another sweltering day. Again, Judy passed the meeting to me. Looking back now, Judy may have been nervous about what might happen this time and that might have added to the pressure. Either way, by the time I got as far as the Tuesday of the induction programme, I could feel the same awful sensation. I had to stop suddenly and, again, put my head in my hands. I think that I got to the Tuesday but, honestly, I can't remember exactly. All I remember is that I managed to speak for a few minutes, but those minutes seemed like a lifetime.

Judy was much more sympathetic this time and her concern for me had clearly been raised by several notches. Once more, I did the walk of shame out of that tiny office and sat in the same room that Judy had directed me to the day before. This time, however, my brain was whirring with the consequences of what had just happened and, unlike the day before, this feeling wasn't going away. I'd had 24 hours to think about it and was beginning to question my whole career. Judy is going to be at least another half an hour, I thought to myself. Should I just leave the building and try to find another job elsewhere? Not unsurprisingly, another terrifying panic attack followed.

I was worried about my job, my career, managing interviews and controlling my breathing. It felt like my very survival was at stake. As I ran through this list in my head, I began to feel quite desperate. Just then Judy bounced into the room, clearly rushing to her next appointment. I was waiting nervously for the verdict on my inability to support her in the interview, but she simply said she hoped that I was ok and that I shouldn't worry because there were no more interviews coming up. And with that, she was off. We never spoke about what happened in those two interviews ever again; it was a subject that we both brushed under the table. Because of that, you'd be forgiven for thinking that Judy played little part in my life after that. It was the opposite, however. We stayed in contact over the years and Judy's daughter was even a bridesmaid at my first wedding. In some ways, that makes the wall of silence we built around those two interviews even more incredible but, as time has gone on, I've come to realise and understand just how hard it is for people to talk openly and easily about moments like this, either as the person in a state of distress or the person witnessing what was going on.

I attended the wedding of my dear friend John the day after those interviews. There's a photograph of me pretending to climb out of a swimming pool wearing a suit. I'm at this wedding doing the very thing that almost everyone associated with me: being the joker in the pack, making people laugh, entertaining everyone and trying to spread as much joy and laughter as possible. But simultaneously, a niggling voice – that demon voice in my mind - was asking endless questions. Should I go back to my job on Monday? Was I going to be fired? How could I be a trainer if I couldn't even speak to people? What was wrong with me? Was I ill? Did I need to see a doctor? But these questions only existed as endless thoughts swirling around my mind because I carried on as if nothing had happened. I told no one and yet the events of those two days haunted me and - if I'm honest - still do.

The photograph I referred to was one of many taken that day. I looked very happy in all of them despite how I felt. Therein lies a critical issue when it comes to our mental health because it's often very hard to know what's really going on with people. Later in the book, I'll run through some simple ways to help you engage with people when they're struggling, but it's often very hard to get people to break their silence. Once you compound that with the understanding that the brightest light will frequently create the darkest shadow, it becomes even more challenging. At that wedding, everyone I met would have thought that my light was shining very brightly. Only I knew the debilitating length and depth of the shadow.

The wall of silence that was created between Judy and me can still be found in organisations everywhere today. It's a metaphor for the way we try to cope with the stigma surrounding mental health. We use the silence to barricade ourselves against the discomfort and embarrassment that engaging with mental ill-health can cause. We've built those walls over years of telling young boys not to cry and thinking that a stiff upper lip is the way to manage these difficulties. Mental health issues have been seen as a source of shame or disgrace and there have been centuries of society and culture convincing itself that showing vulnerability and admitting to mental distress is a sign of weakness. Those ideas, as well as others which will be explored in this book, all contribute to why we have a mental health crisis escalating all around us.

It is time to take down those walls and break the silence.

'Two roads diverged in a wood, and I-
I took the one less travelled by,
And that has made all the difference.'

Robert Frost,
'Road Not Taken'

Chapter 3
Your struggles can be super strengths

Van Gogh, Abraham Lincoln, Virginia Woolf and Elizabeth Gilbert. These are not names you'd often put in the same sentence or associate with a book like this. They are, however, essential to this chapter, because each one demonstrates that sometimes struggles with mental health can become the seed from which the greatest strengths blossom. That was certainly true for me.

Van Gogh, the tormented genius of the art world, grappled with severe depression and anxiety throughout his life. Yet, despite his struggles, he used this to drive his creativity. His ability to channel his struggles into captivating art is a testament to the power of imagination in overcoming adversity. Abraham Lincoln, the stoic leader who steered America through some of its darkest times, battled with melancholy and depression. Yet, it was precisely his struggles with mental health that endowed him with a deep empathy and resilience that cemented his legacy as one of America's greatest presidents.

Throughout her life, Virginia Woolf grappled with bouts of depression and anxiety, which she eloquently chronicled in her writings. Although it took her life eventually, Woolf's struggle became the fuel for her creativity. Through her writing, Woolf explored the complexities that define all of us, paving the way for future generations of writers. Elizabeth Gilbert, the best-selling author of 'Eat Pray Love', struggled with depression and anxiety for much of her life, yet she refused to let her mental health issues hold her back. Instead, she wanted them to be the catalyst for her creativity, channelling her experiences into her writing and turning her struggles into books. Gilbert has inspired millions to embrace their whole self through her candid memoirs and inspirational talks.

Four people whose lives might have been held back by their battles with their mental health. Instead, they chose to turn those battles into super strengths. While I would never put myself in the same category as these artists, the process of discovering how I could turn a struggle into a super strength profoundly affected how I live and work. To explain why, I must take you back to those two fateful interviews - the ones that ended with me having to beat a very hasty retreat due to my panic attacks.

As part of my training the following week, I had to observe various training sessions to get the hang of what a senior trainer did in the company and, just as importantly, how they went about it. Part of my job was to handle induction training for new salespeople in the advertising department and it was clear that this was a crucial part of my development as a trainer. However, my mind was not really focused on the task at hand during these sessions. In truth, I couldn't stop thinking about the previous week and found myself ruminating and going over and over what had happened. It may sound foolish, but I feared my career was ending at just 24.

One of the biggest issues I was struggling with was the question of how I could handle a room of 20 people for several hours if I couldn't even speak to one person for two minutes without the risk of a panic attack? I vividly remember deciding that I would have to quit my job because I couldn't face a repeat of what had happened the week before. I also never wanted the experience of being unable to talk in front of people again. I remember one particular session which dragged on and was so dull that even my self-absorbed and anxiety-ridden brain registered that this was not the most engaging experience. The senior trainer in charge of this session was simply parroting the words on her slides. She read them out to us line by line without interacting with her audience. Time crawled by and I found myself thinking that we could all have just read her notes and done that in a fraction of the time she took to read out every word so laboriously on her slides.

And then it happened. Another moment where my world was turned upside down. I was beginning to think that I had no option but to exit the business and try to work out how I could carve out another career. Judy, however, had other ideas. Tightly clutching the materials used in the session, she came to see me with what she obviously felt was a brilliant opportunity.

'Right, David, it's your turn. You can use these to deliver the induction training in two weeks. It will be great practice for you and I can't wait to see what you can do.'

It's tough to describe how I felt at that moment. The blind panic flooding my body was matched only by the strength of my heart palpitations and I wondered whether I was about to have another panic attack. All I wanted to do was to run away as fast and soon as I could. But I had just started a new job - the training role I had aspired to for some time – and, despite all my thoughts and plans, I hadn't yet quit so I agreed to do it, much to Judy's delight.

I now needed a solution. Should I resign before I had to present in two weeks' time? Or could I feign illness this time to get out of it? For some reason unknown to me, something stopped that cascade of negative thoughts and my professional instinct took over. I decided that I would have to find a way to give the induction training regardless of how I felt. My challenge was to avoid the moments when all eyes were on me. I realised that if I could avoid being the centre of attention in that room, then I might be ok. That's not easy when the job is to be the person all eyes should be on but I knew that if that happened, I would be in dire straits. My previous experiences had shown me that it was highly likely I'd have further panic attacks. But, instead of this being an insurmountable issue, it was the moment my super strength first emerged. Rather than be the centre of attention, I decided to draw the audience's focus away from me. I had a very strong sense that, the more I did that and put the spotlight on the trainees themselves, the more I would protect myself from the onslaught of a panic attack.

I re-wrote the induction programme and simply turned the first session into a quiz. Almost every module was designed to include break-out groups with lots of facilitated group discussions. There was no need to present if I did that and it was easy to manoeuvre the spotlight away from me. This unusual approach raised some eyebrows amongst the more established trainers, but my sessions went really well. As it turned out, the approach I developed to protect myself had a profound effect on the levels of engagement and the overall learning experience of the group with whom I was working. The feedback scores were fantastic and within six months, I was promoted to senior trainer. People described me as a trainer ahead of my time which I thought was laughable. I wasn't particularly innovative, clever or creative; I was just trying to avoid my panic attacks. Little did I know that I had stumbled upon a training style which, 10 years later, would become the norm.

My success in the training role meant I was fast-tracked into senior management and promoted to national sales manager at the relatively young age of 25. A career I thought might be ending had accelerated in the space of only a year because I had found a way to turn adversity into an opportunity, and therefore continued to develop. I wasn't a visionary in terms of employee engagement much as I'd like to claim to be. I used humour and distraction techniques, in effect, to survive each session and this approach became my stock in trade for many years. People saw a leader and presenter innovatively exploring ways of conveying messages in the most engaging way possible. But behind that mask was someone just trying to get through each day without the world realising that I was hiding a secret – the fear and shame of my panic attacks.

I had realised that I was at my most vulnerable at the start of a session and that this was the point when a panic attack was most likely to happen. It was where I most acutely felt the weight of expectation and was most aware of the fixed stare of dozens of eyes waiting for me to speak. Over the years, I've found many ways to offset the danger of a panic attack starting at this point and, for this, I owe a huge thanks to a man called Fish. Mr. Fish was a charismatic and brilliant trainer I encountered many years ago at the start of my career and watching him closely taught me a really valuable lesson. He began his session by saying nothing and simply moving around the room, mimicking fish movements for the first minute. We all watched him, intrigued and slightly bewildered as to what was going on. Training sessions didn't usually start like this. At that point, he revealed his name and promised us that, regardless of the quality of his session, we would never forget him or his name because of the way he had started it. He was right. His entrance distracted from the pressure of the moment and calmed us down; it calmed him down because he knew that we were all intrigued by his bizarre behaviour and any tension we had been feeling was replaced with laughter and curiosity. I thought it was such a simple, brilliant idea that, on the way home that night, I promised myself I'd find a similar solution.

His performance was inspired by his name and I wondered whether my name might also provide a means of disarming my audience. Those who remember the first chapter will already know the answer; I found my salvation in the beans. Since then, I have given out nearly 20,000 tins of baked beans at the start of my sessions. In fact, I've given out so many that Heinz now sponsors me with cans of baked beans which must be a first for a mental health specialist! I'm still touched and inspired by the number of people I meet who tell me that having the tin of beans, which I gave them, sitting slightly incongruously on their desk, has prompted a conversation about why they are there.

Adam Morgan, the strategist, describes the transformation of a limitation into an advantage as a beautiful constraint. My beautiful constraint, that desire to avoid any attention while still delivering important information, meant I had discovered a way of creating engagement by thinking laterally about how to communicate training and key business messages. That had allowed me to become so successful in my various roles that, by the age of 35, I had reached my career goal of being the managing director of a regional daily newspaper. This technique afforded me some respite, but it hadn't solved the underlying issue. I had to wait another 30 years before that happened and, in the meantime, continued to wear the mask which meant no one was aware of the inner turmoil I still frequently felt.

What about you? Do you have a beautiful constraint? You know, the thing that, at first sight looks like a problem, but can be turned into your greatest strength. Maybe it's something you've thought only a little about. Based on my experience, if you do know what it's like to struggle with your mental health, you have already developed a set of skills that will prove to be invaluable, both for you and your workplace.

Those who have navigated mental health struggles often have incredible empathy and understanding toward others facing similar challenges. These skills translate into strong interpersonal skills, making people great communicators, team players, and leaders who can connect with colleagues on a much more meaningful level. Overcoming challenges requires resilience and the ability to adapt to changing circumstances. Individuals who have faced these challenges often possess resilience in the face of adversity, which helps people thrive in an ever-changing work environment. It also allows them to bounce back from setbacks with renewed determination.

As we've seen already, mental health challenges can also foster creativity and innovative thinking as individuals develop coping mechanisms and problem-solving skills to navigate their struggles. They may offer unique perspectives and brilliant solutions to complex problems, contributing to a culture of innovation within their workplace. Through self-reflection and therapy, individuals often develop a high degree of self-awareness and emotional intelligence which are invaluable assets in the modern workplace. They can effectively manage their emotions, navigate interpersonal relationships and make informed decisions that benefit themselves and their teams.

Working around challenges often requires individuals to become resourceful and develop effective time management strategies to balance work and self-care. These skills translate into increased productivity, efficiency and the ability to prioritise tasks effectively. Individuals who have overcome mental health struggles may become advocates for mental health awareness at work. Sharing their experiences and promoting a supportive environment can inspire others to seek help and foster a kinder culture of inclusivity and support.

Finally, dealing with mental health challenges often involves navigating conflicts and negotiating boundaries with yourself and others. Individuals who have honed these skills through their struggles can excel in conflict resolution and negotiation situations in the workplace, fostering positive relationships and effective teamwork. This short list is not exhaustive, but I hope it serves one vital purpose: to illustrate that what we worry about and affects us most significantly can sometimes serve us well.

Despite this, I often reflect on whether finding my beautiful constraint at the age of 24 prevented me from breaking my silence earlier. Had I not discovered a way of hiding my panic attacks by moving the presentation spotlight away from me, I may have had to confront my demons earlier. Of course, you never know; we cannot turn back the clock. The trajectory of my life may have been entirely different if I'd broken my silence in my 20s. As I explained earlier, I don't have answers to these things, but I do know this. My lived experience, and the totality of that experience, makes me more equipped than most to understand and explain why building kinder cultures is the key to looking after your people and your business.

It is time to break the silence.

'Mental pain is less dramatic than physical pain, but it is more common and harder to bear. The frequent attempt to conceal mental pain increases the burden: it is easier to say that my tooth is aching than to say that my heart is broken.'

C. S. Lewis

Chapter 4
Breaking my silence

During my sessions, people ask whether my decision to train as a mental health counsellor and to start my business are linked. In many ways, I wish they had been. There would be a neatness to that, giving the impression that I had formulated a master plan years earlier. Sadly, the reality is a more happenstance chain of events but, in many ways, where I've ended up is all the better for that irregular journey.

By 2008 my employer, Auto Trader, was reorganising its business. An essential part of that process involved an external company helping people leaving the organisation due to the changes. Although it didn't feel like it then, I now realise that Auto Trader was ahead of its time, showing such a duty of care to those who had to think about what was next. And, for many, it was a time of great introspection and consideration about what the future might hold.

Part of my role during this process was to help facilitate the various sessions that were taking place. During one of those sessions, the next and most exciting phase of my career was born. I remember the session well. It was all about purpose. What are we here for? Someone once suggested to me that most people lead lives of quiet desperation and go to their graves with their song still in them. It was a quote they picked up from somewhere I think but it has stayed with me. Maybe, at that point, I subconsciously feared that I was one of those people and it was this that drew me to that session. The first part involved the facilitator going around the table and asking each of us to discuss our purpose. As was often the case in group sessions like this, I was encouraged to go first. But this time, it was for a reason that surprised me. 'Beeney, let's kick off with you. We all know what your purpose is.
So, let's get you out of the way.'

I remember feeling shocked that my purpose was so clear to others when I couldn't really articulate it to myself. The surprise clearly showed on my face.

'Oh, come on, it's so obvious. You're here to make people feel better about themselves. You love it!' someone said.

Everyone around that table agreed. Deep inside, I knew how much I enjoyed developing and inspiring others; I just hadn't ever thought about it as my purpose. In fact, I'd not really ever thought about purpose in the context of my life at all. Years later, I came across the Japanese concept of ikigai, which sums up what the search for purpose truly means. Ikigai represents that moment in your life when you have found a way of simultaneously bringing four critical things together: something you love doing, something you are good at, something you can get paid for and finally, perhaps the most important of all, something the world needs. It's where passion, mission, vocation and profession come together. The word, ikigai, is made up of the Japanese characters which mean 'life' and 'to be worthwhile' and it's best defined as the reason we get up in the morning. Thinking about their ikigai prompts individuals to reflect on what truly motivates them, what they excel at, what the world needs from them and what brings them joy. For some, it can be a guiding principle for decision-making, career choices and overall wellbeing. Anyway, back to the story and what proved to be the first step in that chain of events. There I was, having my eyes opened both to the concept of purpose, which I had not really thought about before and, more tellingly perhaps, my own purpose – something I had definitely not thought about in any meaningful way.

That summer, I was on holiday in Bulgaria. We had gone on a sightseeing trip on what was a searingly hot day. I'd fallen behind the group slightly so ran up some steep steps to catch up. When I got to the top of the steps, out of breath, the air seemed very thin, and I struggled to get my breathing back down. I continued to pant more and more quickly and this, in turn, brought about a panic attack. It was a particularly horrible one. The sort where you can't work out how you're going to stop it, or how you'll ever breathe properly again and where you start to catastrophise and think you'll have a heart attack. Of course, I hid it from the family because I didn't want them to see that I was struggling. The last thing I wanted to do was spoil anything for them, but it did mean that I had a very uncomfortable rest of the holiday.

Whenever I saw a hill or steps ahead, I walked up them very slowly for fear of triggering another episode. I knew I had to get some help because I had no coping mechanism for when it might happen again and, of course, I was now getting panic attacks in my everyday life as well. I loved cycling and often went out with friends on a ride, but it got to the stage where any big hill would induce a panic attack. It wasn't the action of cycling up the hill; just seeing the hill was enough to start the rising wave of anxiety and extreme breathlessness. It had also begun to affect my ability to play squash, up until then one of my favourite sports. I just couldn't imagine how I would be able to run around on a squash court without having a panic attack. It had all become too much and I decided I needed professional help. This decision was to be a defining moment in my life and another step on the journey of events which has brought me to where I am today.

It was the first time since I was in my early 20s that I had been to see anybody about my mental health. Again, I kept my silence and didn't tell my wife I was going to see the doctor. I explained to him what I had been experiencing and he referred me to a counsellor. During one of our sessions, she shared with me that she had been a lawyer but had changed career and was now a mental health counsellor. One day, quite out of the blue, she asked me if I had ever thought about being a counsellor myself.

I think she had become quite interested when she heard about my coping mechanisms and maybe recognised some of the things about me that my work colleagues had also identified. Suffice to say that she told me I could add value as a counsellor and that proved to be the catalyst that led me to train as one whilst I was still at Auto Trader. I will always be grateful to the people around me who, over the years, have pointed me in that direction. Without them and the timing of their interventions, my life would have taken a very different turn.

The penultimate piece in my wellbeing jigsaw came in April 2016. I was still at Auto Trader when somebody in HR approached me and said, 'David, you know a bit about mental health, don't you?'

'I'm not so sure,' I replied somewhat tentatively.

The HR manager then asked about my counselling and I realised why she had asked me the question in the first place. National Mental Health Awareness week was taking place the next month and the company was keen to replace the usual external speaker with someone from within Auto Trader. As a qualified counsellor, HR thought I might fit the bill. I remember the inevitable thoughts racing through my head at the time. Could I get someone to do this presentation for me? How could I get out of doing it myself? I couldn't risk freezing on the day and having a panic attack in front of all my colleagues.

I let the initial conversation go hoping that this was one of those corridor conversations that often go nowhere. You know the ones I mean. An initial idea is born out of enthusiasm but with no real plan and so disappears into the ether. Sadly, how wrong I was. A few days later, I got an email confirming my talks in London and Manchester, requesting the presentation slides a week before the event. As if it wasn't bad enough that the talks had been confirmed, the final line in the email sent a chill down my spine. 'I can't wait to see what you will say.' 'No one will be more surprised than me by what I had to say.' I thought to myself as I read the email. At this stage, it was the princely sum of nothing!

So, I sat down one evening with a blank sheet of paper. Minutes seemed like hours. What am I going to talk about? How on earth am I going to make this engaging? And why would anyone care? Eventually, I rested on the only thing I could usefully do on this topic at this stage: talk about me and my journey. It was the only thing I could discuss with certainty, credibility or honesty. I vowed that night to talk about myself. I was leaving Auto Trader in September of that year, so talking about my battles with mental health was a relatively risk-free decision. It turned out to be one of the best decisions of my life.

Monday, 16 May 2016: exactly eight years to the day before this book was published. It's a date indelibly etched in my memory. The day I first broke my silence and spoke about my story. I got through it without a panic attack and, to my great joy, at the end of my talk, people were queuing up to talk to me and thank me for sharing my story. I witnessed people in tears hearing about my issues and, for the very first time in my life, I realised that my story could help others. For the rest of that week, I did that talk several times in London and Manchester and the enthusiastic, heartfelt response everywhere was the same. But it was at my next talk, in October of that year, that I finally realised where my calling lay and how that sense of purpose that had been lying somewhat dormant in me might be ignited. And, like so many things in my life and career, it didn't happen because of a neat and well-ordered plan. It was thanks to a chance suggestion made by my friend and previous boss, Paul Gibson.

Paul was running a video business and was involved in an event on mental health. He asked if I wanted a ticket because he thought it would be good context for the mental health workshops which I hoped to do to supplement my counselling work. I appreciated his kind thought and told him I'd love to go. It felt like an opportunity for some fascinating new learning for me. Little did I know what was to follow and the impact it would have on the direction of my life. A few days after making his offer, Paul rang to explain that he had secured a ticket for me but there was a proviso.

'What's that?' I asked nervously.

He then explained that my ticket for the event was on the proviso that I delivered a 45-minute talk on the topic while I was there. I'll never know whether this was his way of throwing me in at the deep end but doing this proved to be the final stage of my metamorphosis. I can remember being outside the room, physically shaking with fear. I knew that the upcoming hour could be one of the most important of my life. If I could engage a room of nearly 100 HR directors, I could go on to build something.

The rest, as they say, is history. People loved what I said and I'm still in touch professionally with some of the people I met that day. My new business was born. All I needed now was a name for it. And the more I thought about it, the more obvious it was what I should call that business. Telling my story meant I had broken my silence and, in turn, I wanted to help other people to break theirs. It was only a small creative leap then to work out the name of my new business. Breaking The Silence, the thing that proved to be the best decision of my professional life, was born.

I had broken my silence and it was now time to help others break theirs.

Chapter 5
Can you measure your mental health?

Before we tackle the answer to this chapter's title, I want to tell you about Sally, her dogs and Sharon. That might sound like the start of one of those jokes you overhear in the pub but, in this instance, it's the start of a story that has taught me some life-changing lessons on my wellbeing journey. Sharon was my boss and Sally worked as part of our team. One day, out of the blue, Sharon asked me a question that I'll never forget.

'How is Sally's dog?' she said. I laughed nervously as people often do when confronted with something out of their comfort zone. Sharon asked what was funny in the direct manner I'd become accustomed to from a very straight-talking sales director.

'Sorry,' I said, shuffling uncomfortably as I explained that I wasn't sure why she'd asked, given that I didn't even know Sally had a dog. Her reply was calm and very matter of fact.

'Well, David,' she continued. 'You should know that Sally has a dog and that dog is her life. If you want to connect with Sally on any meaningful level, you'll need to ask about the dog; it's a non-negotiable subject matter.'

Sharon had put me firmly in my place and I decided to take her advice when I next chatted to Sally. Of course, as Sharon had known, her advice worked. Sally lit up as soon as I asked her about the canine love of her life and she was as animated as I'd ever seen her. To add weight to Sharon's approach, I remember being at the Henley School of Management some years ago where a Japanese CEO shared his most important advice for leaders. He told us that he had eight direct reports and would ensure that he spoke to all of them at least every other day but that only half of those conversations would be about work. As I looked around the room, I saw some disappointment from my fellow students who were expecting more sophisticated advice. However, I loved its simplicity and its focus on the importance of knowing your team as human beings first and work colleagues second. 'Be more human' is a good mantra for how we should all lead our lives.

More recently, a very senior leader who, by his own definition, could be described as an alpha male called me to give me a story that he felt I could use in my workshops. I've included it in this book because it tells you all you need to know about the importance of building relationships at work that have nothing to do with work. Here was a man who, for almost all his career, had felt that conversations about anything other than work or business were a waste of time and the refuge of the inefficient underachiever. That is until his light bulb moment.

That moment involved a team member who had always been very uncomfortable in his presence for the two years she had worked with him. You can picture the scene: always little eye contact, often darting the other way to avoid him and always a rushed mumble when asked a question. All of that changed because of one seminal moment. Having heard that his team member had recently taken a day off work to settle her son back at university, our alpha leader asked about her son the next time they met in the corridor. Within minutes, and after an incredibly engaged conversation, they wandered to the kitchen to make coffee and to chat further about their children. It was the first time they had ever spoken about something that wasn't directly related to work. The result? A transformed relationship and a team member who quickly became more engaged, more productive and happier.

There's no blinding insight in those stories because we all instinctively know that to build meaningful relationships, you must connect with people on a very human level. The pandemic helped that process for reasons we all know. But, and here's the rub, how many of us can say that we are genuinely interested in the lives of the people we work with? Do we know what inspires and excites them and where their hopes and dreams lie? Many years ago, I overheard a conversation between two people keen to understand how to get the best out of their teams. 'You have to understand what everybody's melody is,' one said to the other. 'You know, the thing that lights their fire.'

At the time, I remember thinking that finding someone's melody was an excellent thought for any leader. In the context of where the theory of leadership is heading today, authenticity and bringing your whole self to work will always separate the good from the great. Just a side note here: I know I've just used the phrase 'bringing your whole self to work' and that is something we often hear these days. However, I have never been entirely sure about that idea. My view is that it's far better to bring your whole self to life and let work follow. I see this in the leadership teams with whom I interact. Those leaders who show genuine vulnerability make faster, more meaningful progress with their teams than those who don't because they connect better and so build deeper, more resilient relationships, something I'm going to discuss further later in the book.

Back to Sharon for a moment. Aside from knowing what the melodies of her team were, she also had an instinct for another incredible weapon. She knew the importance of creating structured time for unstructured conversations, a phrase you might remember from earlier on and something I'd like to focus on further. Don't get me wrong, Sharon was a demanding boss. She could be fierce when she wanted but she was very successful. You felt part of a real work family if you worked for Sharon. We knew a lot about each other and cared about each other. Sharon led a three-hour monthly sales meeting that often had us quaking in our boots. It was not a meeting to be in if your numbers weren't good. But the funny thing is that she always started that meeting with a check-in with all of us which focused on non-work matters.

There was one occasion where, for diary reasons, we only had 90 minutes instead of the usual three hours and with a longer agenda than usual. Inevitably one of the team suggested that we got straight down to business in order not to waste time and to get through everything. But that wasn't Sharon's way.

She valued her team time too much.

'No way,' she said emphatically. 'I find out more about all of you in that first half an hour than I do for the rest of the month. That bit stays.'

And with that, the die was cast. Sharon would never discard her secret weapon because it created greater engagement within our team than anything else we did. The things Sharon taught me didn't stop there. She was a leader well ahead of her time in so many ways and she saved her most important lesson until last. It's the one I've used most in my work and has proved to be as powerful as it is transformative over recent years.

We were a team scattered far and wide, all living and working in different parts of the UK. Because of this, the Monday morning conference calls were a big part of our week. Those calls always started the same way. Every team member had to give a score out of 10 for how they were feeling. While working in Sharon's region, I often sat beside her on the calls. Every week, I noticed that she would write all the scores down. Being naturally curious, I remember asking Sharon why she did that. Her answer was both simple and brilliant in equal measure.

'David,' she said, 'You'll find that most people always give the same score. Kevin's always an eight, Darren's always a seven. Sarah's always a seven, too,' she continued whilst scribbling on her notepad. 'What I'm interested in, is variation. If anyone suddenly gives a lower score, I know something's wrong.'

Sharon then explained that if she encountered a lower number, she would follow up with that person during the day to check in with them. I remember one person vividly from that time and how significant this notion of a score out of 10 was for him. His name was Gary and, to be honest, he was annoying. He had more front than Blackpool and more rabbit than Sainsbury's. And he was always a 10 in every meeting except one week, when he scored himself a nine. I nearly fell off my chair and inwardly smiled at how his life was falling apart. Oh, to be only a nine, I thought to myself. However, I quickly regretted taking Gary's scores so lightly. As we subsequently discovered, his life was beginning to fall apart and Gary left the business some weeks later because of his struggles.

It became clear to me that Gary's nine was someone else's five and that it was the drop from his usual 10, rather than the fact he was still a nine, that we should have taken more seriously. As was so often the case, Sharon was right; look out for variation because this might indicate a change in someone's wellbeing. It was a powerful reminder of how personal a journey everyone's wellbeing is. I use the score out of 10 as part of my work now and, as we all settle into a new hybrid working world, this simple way of checking on how someone is feeling has become so much more important. Hybrid working has many benefits but there are some equally important watchouts. Many leaders I've met use hybrid working as a flimsy excuse for being unable to keep an eye on how their people and colleagues are. They argue that the virtual environment is a less personal and less engaging one because people aren't in the same physical space. Of course that brings its challenges, but I disagree that it's less personal and here's why. I've met more dogs, cats, children and partners in those virtual meetings in recent years than I did over the last 30 or 40 years. In some ways there is less of a division between home and work life now and we can use this to find ways to connect when we're not sitting in an office together.

It's also about having your cameras on when you're in meetings if possible, so you can see each other and so you can connect. And not worrying about the fact that working from home is not exactly like working in an office. I see too many people trying to be too corporate with incredibly dull backdrops. Suppose the pet cat jumps on the keyboard? Let's meet it and find out its name. If a child walks past in the background, let's say hello. What's wrong with seeing into each other's lives occasionally? We should all work harder in the new working world to get to know each other personally because we know how meaningful those human connections are. Sometimes, those connections can help people hugely as they did in one session which I remember particularly clearly. It's not unusual for me to have up to 100 people in one of my workshops and often I'm presenting for much of the time. So it was on this occasion. At the end of the session, the client who had organised the event asked me how I thought it had gone. I told her it had gone very well but, as a duty of care, I gave her the names of three people on the webinar that I thought she needed to check in with. She looked at me, slightly puzzled, and asked how I could have identified those three people from the nearly 90 people in the session, most of whose cameras were off.

I explained that one of the things I got people to do on the call was to type a number between one and 10 in the chat function to score how they felt that day. The three people in question only rated themselves a one which could have been a cry for help. It turned out to be so for two of those people and, because of the follow-up the company could do, additional support was put in place for them. But what of the third person? When HR checked in on them, they said they were actually a 10 and that this was just a keyboard error because they'd forgotten to add the zero!

Why out of 10 and what exactly are you measuring? For a start, wellbeing and the stigma surrounding mental health are global issues. Nowadays, my sessions are in different countries and different continents every day, but we all understand the language of one to 10. We all know seven out of 10 is ok and we also know that eight or nine is good. Anything under seven indicates that you could feel that you have less energy than usual. Even children have an excellent understanding of the idea of one to 10. I had an incredibly thoughtful email from a mum recently telling me she had used the scoring technique with her daughter after one of my sessions. How she responded led to one of the most honest and open conversations she'd ever had with her child about the daughter's wellbeing. Moments like that remind me of my purpose and give me even greater motivation to continue my journey.

There's a clear relationship between your energy, mental resilience and stamina. No one needs to read a book on this subject to know that how much energy you have affects almost everything you do daily. But the key, of course, is for us not to track solely how we are feeling on any given day. If you'd asked me about my score out of 10 on different days this week, you'd have got scores ranging from five to about nine depending on which day it was. Your daily scores will go up and down but it's the overall trend that matters most. It's this which will determine whether you can make progress or not. And that progress depends on having meaningful ways to measure it. Those of us in business instinctively know that. It's why it's much easier to focus on our physical health. We have tech that measures physical health. Our Fitbit or Garmin can tell us how many steps we've taken, what our resting heart rate is, how many hours we've slept and how much weight we've lost (or gained) over the past month. We know that the things we focus on improve more effectively, and making these improvements is so much easier for our physical health, where there are these clear measurements.

It's harder to have indicators in the context of wellbeing so the score out of 10 measure is an important one. As Sharon taught me, it can reveal meaningful variations for leaders who are interested in finding ways to support their teams. For individuals, it's a helpful way to continually check in with yourself and give you a broad measure of your feelings by looking at the overall pattern. But the fact that so many people don't believe you can measure your mental health means we still have a long way to go. We need a new age of enlightenment around one to 10 and we all need to find more useful ways to measure wellbeing.

This topic is the subject of our next chapter because that which you pay attention to grows. Far too many of us sleepwalk into ignoring the things that best determine how well we feel. If we focus on this much more, we will all be able to tackle the daily slings and arrows life throws at us. We do owe that to ourselves and to the people who love us most.

It is time to measure our wellbeing to help break the silence.

'It seems to me that the natural world is the greatest source of excitement; the greatest source of visual beauty; the greatest source of intellectual interest. It is the greatest source of so much in life that makes life worth living.'

Sir David Attenborough

Chapter 6
52 out of 60

You'll now understand the importance of your score out of 10. But many of you may need help on what to measure beyond the broad overall score. It's a crucial question and one this chapter will answer.

But before I do that, let's rewind the clock to 2014. The year the world first saw the ice bucket challenge: the viral sensation where participants dumped a bucket of ice over their heads for charity. It was also the year that Tim Vine picked up the award for the funniest joke of the Edinburgh fringe: 'I've decided to sell my Hoover.... well, it was just gathering dust.' I'm known for my love of a good one-liner so I couldn't resist including at least one dad joke in this book. You'll be pleased to hear it's the only one. 2014 was also the year that Pharrell Williams claimed the honour of the biggest single of the year with 'Happy'.

Except, I was anything but happy. 2014 was probably the worst year of my life. My fear of my panic attacks was at its worst and I thought my career was finished. The revelation that enabled me to start 'Breaking The Silence' was still two years in the future and I was enduring a torrid and very difficult time trying to manage my mental health struggles in silence. My colleagues were often baffled about why I appeared to hold myself back in meetings. If only they had known what I was going through. Worse than that, my 28-year marriage was coming to an end.

The emotional and financial impact was enormous. I could not see a way of ever bouncing back. I felt considerable guilt for the hurt I was inflicting on my children and now ex-wife and a very deep and profound sadness. I'd lost my home and some of my friends and I had gone back to live with mum and dad, aged 52. If there are ways to make you feel that your life is at its lowest ebb, I was collecting them all at once. Life was truly shit.

I remember someone once telling me that the darkest hour is always before the dawn and never was that truer than for me at that time. Even in that darkest hour, I knew I needed to regain control of my life and put myself back on the path towards happiness.

So, I sat down one day to determine what made me happiest and why. It was the only way I could think of to help me reset and it involved a vast amount of soul searching. What made me truly happy, what fulfilled me and what most impacted my energy and wellbeing? It wasn't a question that was easy to answer. I had to be very honest about what mattered to me and what didn't. I knew this wasn't a moment to try and kid myself. It forced me to reflect that time and life are both finite. As the saying goes, no one is getting out of here alive. And yet, we all treat time and life as if they are infinite. We make the mistake of believing that we can fit ever more into our days and weeks and that one day, we will learn to sing, take up golf or live our purpose. We spend our days prioritising what we must get done rather than what we love doing or what gives our lives meaning. I often refer to this as the busy zone in a corporate context. I see people at work spending their days busy rather than understanding where they can make the most significant impact and then intentionally focusing on those things.

Anyway, let's get back to that period of soul searching, during which I worked out which six parts of my life determined my happiness and were the things I needed to focus on. They were my physical health, mental health, financial wellbeing, the clarity of my purpose, my family and the critical relationship in my life (such that I had one at this stage). I gave each of those six areas a mark out of 10 based on how they were at that point of my life. Eight years later, I still review and score them every couple of months. I make time for that process because it matters and you should make time for it as well. I will return to the specifics of my list in a minute but, before I do, I wanted to explain why the regular check-in works. As I've said before, what you pay attention to grows and keeping everything in sync is almost impossible. But having a regular check-in on your list lets you see what you need to focus on and what's going well. Think of this list as the mental health equivalent of your Fitbit. Use it to give yourself the best chance to look after the things that matter to you.

Back to the specifics of my list. The critical word in that sentence is 'my' because everyone's list will differ. Sure, some things are non-negotiable like your physical wellbeing, but don't be afraid to list the things that matter to you. One of mine is purpose, and whilst we are all best served by knowing where we are heading in life, that's not always clear to people. So, clarifying or defining your purpose may not be for you at this stage. As a parent, I know you are only as happy as your unhappiest child, which means that how my family is doing is a significant determinant of my wellbeing. And so it goes on; each to their own, as they say. The only important thing is defining your list and checking your score out of 10 on a regular basis. So, the next time someone asks how you are, try saying '50, thanks' and see how they react. At the very least, it will prompt a conversation about what that number means and why having a score out of 10 matters.

Remember me saying it was vital not to kid yourself about these measures? I know this for certain given my experience with one of my best mates a few years after I had made my list. One evening we met for a drink, as we often do, and I thought it was high time I introduced him to my way of measuring my mental health. By this time, I felt more chipper about life and happy to score myself. Having asked how I was, he was somewhat taken aback by my answer of 52. I then explained why and left him to get some drinks. By the time I came back, my mate had given it some thought and asked me to elaborate on the individual scores, which I did. As I ran through them, he questioned every score, asking whether I had been viewing my life through a pair of heavily tinted rose-coloured glasses. His analysis seemed harsh as he then went through the list, but his point was made from a place of genuine friendship. And, as it transpired, he was right. I was kidding myself about some of the scores. We all do it.

At one level, it's called putting a brave face on. At another level, it's about not being prepared to face where we find ourselves at that point in life's journey. But we must be honest about the starting point to know which path to take and the honesty forced on me in that moment by someone who cared about me, helped me make better decisions about what to do next. So, this is a Beeney mental health warning to say that measuring your mental health is something you can do, but you owe it to yourself to be honest about where your starting point is and how you assess your scores regularly.

At this point, it's worth briefly examining some of my six measures in case they prove a useful springboard for you to think about yours. As a reminder, mine were physical health, mental health, financial wellbeing, clarity of purpose, my family and the critical relationship in my life and, as I said, yours may or may not be like this list. While it may be obvious to include physical health, this book is not a guide to optimising that element. However, I would always include the importance of sleep in this context because this also has a huge impact on our mental wellbeing.

What do I mean when I talk about my second area, mental health? We all instinctively know how we feel, think and behave. Those three things affect every aspect of our lives. We also instinctively know when some of those things are out of kilter. If you feel they are, then that's what I mean about your mental health suffering. Only you can judge that, but I know that solutions such as mindfulness, meditation and counselling can help build your mental resilience and emotional intelligence. Financial wellbeing mattered because I knew that anxiety around finances and money had a big impact on how I felt about life. However, it had also become increasingly clear to me that clarity of purpose plays a vital role in shaping one's sense of meaning and fulfilment. Part of my issue had been that I was not clear about my purpose and that my life, therefore, was not aligned with that purpose. I had to be honest about my values, passions and goals. Going through that process was challenging but it gave me both direction and motivation to rebuild and foster a sense of purpose beyond just material success. In your case, whether that purpose involves pursuing a meaningful career, engaging in something creative or contributing to causes more significant than yourself, try and find it because it will make a huge difference.

Lastly, my family relationships are fundamental to my wellbeing and I include what I termed my 'critical relationship' in this category. Not only do these relationships provide love, support and a sense of belonging but they also foster trust, communication and mutual understanding. Spending quality time together with my family and partner, expressing gratitude for those relationships and constructively resolving the conflicts that naturally arise as part of family life are all things that help me feel better about myself.

As I said, I'm not being prescriptive in any way about the measures you choose. They should be as unique to you as your DNA. It's essential to spend time thinking about what they are and it's even more critical that they reflect the things that matter to you. If they don't, they won't be relevant and won't help you gain perspective on your life or help you measure your wellbeing effectively. You don't have to have six and you don't need to mark them every week. The point is to have some and then to check in on them regularly.

There's one final reason why these metrics matter. Physical health is relatively easy to monitor. We all know when we have a stomach ache or pain in our joints. We all know what to do if we inadvertently cut ourselves while cooking or wake up with a temperature. We either patch it up, take a tablet or visit the doctor. And here's the curious thing about doctors. If we see one and they prove unhelpful or we don't like the cut of their jib, our instinct is not to question whether we ever go back to see a doctor again. We find another one in our area or within our existing GP practice. And yet, I've met many people who have been to see a counsellor, didn't like that individual or the way they worked and then never tried counselling or therapy again. In doing so, some people who may need it miss out on valuable support, guidance and coping strategies that could help them navigate their challenges and improve their mental health.

These last two chapters were designed to give you food for thought about how we might measure our mental health. Like many of the concepts in this book, it's about a shift in mindset to one that values prioritising wellbeing. If you are reading this book as a leader, perhaps consider this. Would you ever dream of starting the year without a clear set of objectives to build the health of your business? Of course not, and neither would you ignore the regular measurement of those objectives. So why is it any different for the people working with you? In the end, you treasure what you measure, so let's make the way we measure our mental health something we all take more seriously.

It's time to treasure what we measure to help break the silence.

Chapter 7
One in one

To be or not to be, that is the question according to one of the greatest playwrights. Compared to Hamlet's question, the one I frequently have to confront may seem more mundane, but it still vexes many of the companies I work with regarding the sessions I run for them. To be mandatory, or not to be mandatory; that is their question. It's not an easy one to answer but it might be worth laying out the case either way for any leader thinking about this issue.

Mandatory mental health sessions play a vital role in raising awareness and de-stigmatising mental health issues. By making the sessions mandatory, companies signal their commitment to prioritising employee wellbeing. It becomes something so important that the organisation commits everyone's time and attention to actively working on wellbeing. In doing so, they create a culture of openly discussing mental health, reducing the fear of judgement and the likelihood of discrimination. These sessions can also provide employees with valuable coping strategies, stress management techniques and resources for seeking help when needed. By addressing mental health proactively, companies can reduce absenteeism, turnover rates and workplace conflicts, improving productivity and overall job satisfaction.

However, there is another perspective and one which raises valid concerns about the effectiveness and practicality of making mental health sessions mandatory. The argument here is that forcing employees to participate may inadvertently exacerbate feelings of discomfort or resentment, particularly among those who prefer to address their mental health privately. Mandatory sessions may also fail to accommodate the diverse needs of employees because individuals experience mental health issues differently. Additionally, some worry about the potential for sessions to be perceived as insincere gestures by employers rather than genuine efforts to support employee wellbeing.

There is no right or wrong answer here other than to say that, in my experience, many of the issues around making the sessions mandatory are quickly forgotten if the sessions are handled sensitively and provide practical solutions to support individuals.

Some of the most impactful sessions I've run were mandatory for men, especially blue-collar workers who might not have attended otherwise. While they may not have shown immediate enthusiasm, some later reached out to me privately to express their gratitude, saying that the session was the best hour spent in the company in decades and occasionally even stating that doing this had potentially saved their lives. Mandating sessions can sometimes be the only way to engage specific demographics, particularly men, and sometimes the only way to break the silence is to ensure that you get everyone together to understand why that silence is so damaging. Those least likely to be able to speak out and break their silence are often those least likely to come to a voluntary session. It's also important that everyone in an organisation understands this issue because it takes everyone to break that silence.

We must normalise discussions around mental health, which is why so many pages of my book are dedicated to this issue. An interesting example illustrates how far we still need to go to do this. Sometimes in my sessions, I will liken the topic to conversations about our physical health. I'll ask the audience what images they might find on Google for physical health. The answers are always the same: elite athletes with bodies to admire, people who work out regularly and who look in peak condition. They are the images that the words 'physical health' conjure up. However, when I ask the same question about images associated with 'mental health', the typical response tends to involve sombre depictions of distress and suffering: people with their heads in their hands, faces fraught with sadness and despair, or symbolic images of dark clouds. This stark contrast underscores the disparity in how society perceives mental health compared to physical health. It also exemplifies how far we have to travel before we remove the stigma of mental health.

Numbers are never in short supply when it comes to this subject. If you believe what you read, one in four people will experience a mental health problem each year in England. One in six people report experiencing a common mental health problem, such as anxiety and depression. And, in any given week in England, eight in 100 people suffer mild anxiety and depression, six in 100 people suffer generalised anxiety disorder and three in 100 people suffer depression. One in five people have suicidal thoughts throughout their lifetime, one in 14 people self-harm and one in 15 people attempt suicide. Finally, approximately only one in eight adults with a mental health problem is getting any treatment. Manage to keep up with all those stats? No, me neither. They often feel like an unnecessary bombardment of the senses. Numbers are referenced with little or no context, giving the feeling of a situation largely out of control. I don't think any of these numbers help us break the silence. In fact, I worry that they may have the opposite effect.

You can find organisations everywhere regularly quoting these statistics. Please understand that I know they mean well and are all trying to help. However, this fixation on numbers is a significant part of the problem and rarely part of the solution. Perhaps the most often quoted number comes from Mind, the mental health charity for whom I was a trustee and one I greatly respect. It constantly refers to the 'one in four' statistic I mentioned above and the implication is evident. You see four people together and wonder which one is the one with the mental health problem. Equally, if you think you are that one in four, it becomes almost impossible to speak out and be different from the other three. No one wants to feel that they are the odd one out. There is, of course, another flaw with the 'one in four' number; what about those who suffer in silence and whose distress is not picked up and recorded? For many years, I was one of the invisible statistics.

No one knew that I had issues and, every year, I have hundreds of people explaining to me how long they have been suffering in silence. How can they be part of the often-quoted numbers when no one knew about thems? When you realise this, you understand how unhelpful the quoted numbers are.

We must change our mindset about how we relate to these numbers around mental health. I'm highly suspicious of almost every number I see because my experience is that the only true number is one in one. Let me explain what I mean by that. To normalise how we feel about our wellbeing, we must understand that we all have physical and mental health. On some occasions, our physical health isn't excellent. We drink too much, sit too long, don't sleep well or tweak a muscle. It happens to everyone. The only difference is that it happens at different times for all of us. It's precisely the same with our mental health.

We know that our physical health is fluid and changeable and that we will inevitably have issues with it at some point in our lives. Imagine if I stood in front of a room of people and asked them whether they knew that one in four adults would experience some form of physical health issue in any given year. They'd probably look at me strangely and quickly point out how ridiculous an assertion that was. Who doesn't stub a toe, cut a finger, catch a cold, or get a nasty headache? We usually manage these health problems and injuries ourselves and only seek professional help when we need something beyond our resources: a course of antibiotics, a stitch for a deep cut or to check that those headaches aren't symptoms of something more sinister. This is precisely the case with our mental health. I don't need to have a diagnosis of depression to have days when my mental health is not brilliant. It is not one in four of us but all of us.

There isn't an 'us' and a 'them' but, in reality, an 'all of us'; at some point all of us will have had a sense that our mental health is not the best it could be. Some of us suffer more chronically than others, and some suffer more acutely; some people receive formal diagnoses and others just muddle through, trying to cope the best that they can. The quicker we understand that point, the more we will remove the stigma felt by those people who cannot talk about what they're going through. They think that they are the one in four when they nervously shuffle into my sessions and that everyone else is – for want of a better word - normal. In doing this, we can even remove the need for the debate around mandatory or voluntary. Looking after your mental health should be as everyday a thing to do as eating, breathing, exercising, loving and laughing. It is part and parcel of life on earth; the quicker we normalise it, the better the world will be. We should all ensure we look after it every day and know that there will be days when, just as our knee might hurt if we've tripped and fallen, we might feel a little under the weather. During those days, we need to remind ourselves that compassion begins at home and that we can't hope to care for others if we do not care for ourselves. People often ask me what that looks like when it comes to our mental health, so I'll finish this chapter with some thoughts on ways I've seen people taking care of themselves over the years and the difference that doing these things makes. Perhaps there are some ideas or approaches here that you could try.

Most importantly, stop punishing yourself for your mistakes. Accept that you are not perfect and be gentle with yourself when confronted with your shortcomings. It's a truism that your closest friends value you because of who you are and not because you are faultless or perfect. A straightforward way to help yourself is to put a sticky note near your desk or in your wallet to remind you to be gentle and kind to yourself today. Then talk to yourself in the way you would speak to someone you care about. You'll be amazed at the difference that simple reminder makes.

Years of research prove the importance and impact of our mindset on wellbeing. Carol Dweck's work in this area shows that whether we have a fixed or growth mindset influences our happiness. Do you view challenges as impossible obstacles or as opportunities to grow? Is the obstacle there because you are not capable of the task or simply because you haven't yet learned how to overcome it or found the way round it? Employing a growth mindset is a very helpful way to nurture your wellbeing. Embrace rather than avoid challenges, persist in finding meaning in them and don't give up on yourself. Understand that we are all capable of learning and changing and that failing at something is part of the learning process rather than a statement of ability. Rather than criticising yourself and negatively comparing yourself with others, try to find inspiration in their successes and strengths instead of feeling threatened. I worked in an industry for years that was dreadful at this. Sometimes, I got the feeling from my colleagues that a little piece of them died when other people were successful. It was partly the era, but it was also the industry. Competition and winning were all and this very binary, zero-sum game attitude was about as helpful to your sense of wellbeing as a chocolate fireguard.

Feeling gratitude is also very powerful. Rather than wishing for what we do not have, there is strength in appreciating what we have right now. You can choose to write a gratitude journal or go for gratitude walks. I have a friend who finishes their day by simply writing five words that sum up the things that have been inspiring or engaging in that day. In his quieter moments, I know he looks back on those words to remind himself of the many positive feelings and experiences over recent months. For him, those five little words are a literal and metaphorical journey. By focusing on what we have, we employ a gentler inner voice and move that focus away from our shortcomings and onto what is good in our lives.

I'll share a quick story here just to illustrate what I mean. I remember a day in 2018 when I was in the car on my way to see my mum who had been admitted to hospital for pneumonia. I remember clearly how sorry I was feeling for myself as I listed all the things that I was having to cope with. As well as my mum being so unwell, my dad was in a care home suffering from Alzheimer's. As a result, we had just had to cancel our summer holiday and, to cap it all, my partner Lisa was ill with a painful kidney infection. As I drove along the road to the hospital absorbed in all my worries, I rang Lisa partly to see how she was feeling but also because I was hoping for a bit of sympathy given how I was feeling. I got nothing of the sort. Instead, Lisa gave me a good kick up the backside reminding me that, although things were tough, I had a considerable amount to be grateful for and that I should be focusing on that. Why am I telling you this story? The following day, I found myself on the exact same stretch of road, again off to visit my mum who was still no better.

The difference this time was that I was feeling pretty good about life. Nothing had changed other than Lisa helping me rediscover the value of gratitude. Looking at what was good in my life - which included having her as part of it - changed the way I was feeling. I wonder how many of us could do with a Lisa in our lives now and again, just to remind us to appreciate what we have rather than to ruminate on what we don't have.

They say that there are two types of people in the world. Some make it halfway up the mountain and look up, only to worry about how far they have left to go. And some, having travelled to that point, look down and marvel at how far they have come. Those people are the ones who stop and smell the flowers along the way during their lives. And these people have the very best chance of being kinder to themselves. Celebrate what you have rather than what you don't have. Remind yourself of the people around you who love you dearly. Please pick up the phone to someone who has made a big difference to your week and thank them spontaneously. You'll make their week better and you'll also feel good about yourself. Stopping to smell those flowers will also allow you to slow down, something else we don't value but which can help our mental health.

We could all benefit from being slow coaches these days. Slowing down doesn't mean giving up ambition or productivity; it simply allows you to find a healthy balance. The slow coaches I know take time to pause, breathe and relax which they tell me helps lower their stress hormones. When I slow down, I often have my best ideas. Creativity flourishes best when you're not constantly rushing from one task to another. I remember being told off in school for daydreaming, but allowing your mind to slow down and wander can stimulate your creative thinking and problem-solving abilities. Believe it or not, daydreaming can be good for you. Perhaps most importantly, rushing through life can lead to neglecting the people who most matter to you. Slowing down allows you to invest time and energy in your relationships, fostering stronger and deeper connections with your friends and family. It enables us to be more present and attentive in the moments that matter. Moments that very often you can't have back. Let's hear it for the slow coaches.

And finally, it's also worth mentioning the power of nature. Just getting outside, amongst trees and plants, is another great way of being kinder to ourselves. Reminding ourselves of the sheer beauty of what is around us helps enormously. Even a quick walk in your local park and appreciating that experience can help shift your mood.

So, a chapter which demonstrates that mental health challenges are as universal as the need for food and water. Ultimately, we are all subject to the peaks and valleys of emotions and these affect one in one of us. And while I hope that this chapter has given you some ideas on how to look after yourself and be kinder to yourself for your own mental wellbeing, I passionately believe there is another important reason for doing this. The more we can look after ourselves, the more we can hope to look after others. That journey must start from within and, for that reason alone, we should always start with our wellbeing.

It is time to break our own silence first.

Chapter 8
Creating kinder cultures

One cold morning, American psychologist Elizabeth Dunn asked people walking down a street in the Canadian city of Vancouver to participate in an experiment. They were given an envelope containing either a $5 or $20 note. Half the people were instructed to spend the money on themselves. The other half were asked to use the money to buy a present for someone else or to donate the money to charity. In both cases, they had until five o'clock that day to spend the money.

That evening, the researchers spoke to all the participants. The first group said they'd bought various things for themselves, such as sushi, earrings or coffee. People from the second group bought toys for their relatives and edible gifts or gave money to homeless people in the street. The researchers then asked each participant to rate their mood. The results were fascinating and the subject of this chapter. They say that kindness wins, which was undoubtedly true on that cold Vancouver morning.

Whether those people had $5 or $20 made no difference, nor did what they had bought. What mattered was who they spent their money on. The people who had spent it on someone else felt significantly happier than those who spent it on themselves.

I'm not suggesting that the key to kindness revolves around spending money on others. But, as it turns out, doing good for others, looking after others rather than focusing on ourselves means everyone benefits, because it helps the wellbeing of those being kind too. Everyone wins when kindness is viewed as a strength at work and actively encouraged. The critical question is how you create those kinder cultures, and I'd like to explain three ways that can consistently happen.

At the heart of this is what happens at the top of any organisation. Culture always eats strategy for breakfast. To develop and maintain a culture of kindness, it must start at the very top. A fish rots from its head and I've seen so many examples over the years of where leaders get it wrong and far fewer where they get it right.

However, at the beginning of the pandemic, I witnessed a leader who understood the importance of authenticity, compassion and putting wellbeing at the heart of his organisation. Back in 2004, Andy Alderson launched Vanarama as a used vehicle retailer before moving into the leasing of commercial vehicles in 2007. It's a business he lived and breathed for over 20 years, one in which the ability to sell and relentlessly focus on customer service is critical. But his message to his business in April 2020 was unequivocal.

'At the moment, I don't care about sales.' he stated. 'All I care about is you and your families' wellbeing.' He then told his teams that he would put his energy into ensuring that the business emerged better and stronger from the pandemic and that he was excited at the prospect of trying to pivot the company in this new world. And so, in one stroke, Andy built more loyalty, showed more empathy and demonstrated greater authenticity than at almost any time in the history of Vanarama. Of course, Andy cared about sales and, of course, he wanted the business to grow. But, at that moment, he also wanted his teams to know he cared more about them. The result? Sales went up, his customer satisfaction scores went up and the business flourished. So much so that in March 2022, Auto Trader acquired Vanarama in a deal that was reported to be worth up to £200 million. He remains one of the humblest yet most talented leaders I know. Who says that wellbeing isn't a commercial lever?

Employees quickly spot companies that don't care. I was working with a client a few years ago and the first piece of work I ever did for them was a talk to about 70 people. When we got to the Q&A, one of the team put their hand up and asked why none of the senior management were at the session.

At the back of the room, a solitary voice said, 'They're just busy.' The room fell silent and everyone understood the implication of what was being said. They weren't 'just busy'. They weren't interested and their absence spoke volumes. It set the tone for how wellbeing was perceived in the organisation. What you pay attention to grows (you'll notice that I like that phrase!) and this was not an organisation that paid any attention to how its people felt or what role wellbeing played in their ability to perform at their best. Sadly, this is not an unusual scenario and is a subject I will shine a light on in a later chapter.

The second key to building kinder cultures is to ensure that anyone in the organisation responsible for people understands the immense responsibility they carry to nurture, support and care for the people in their team. Helping people become the best version of themselves can be life-changing and the best leaders I know create an environment where this is possible.

We've all had a boss that hoovers up the mood in any room and we understand how debilitating it is to wake up every morning dreading your first interaction with that person. We can all spot the derailers. What do I mean by that? Well, the behaviours that can derail almost all leaders. Arrogance, volatility, the love of melodrama, habitual distrust, aloofness and passive resistance are just a few. As you read this list, I'm sure you've had flashbacks, matching names and faces to those who've demonstrated those derailers. Perhaps you recognise some of these behaviours in yourself if you're a leader?

This book is a rallying cry for all of us to break the silence. So, if you're reading this as someone responsible for people with lots of direct reports themselves, spend time and money training your leaders. Teach them to overcome some of their derailers to help them support and nurture others. A kinder culture is one in which we all prioritise helping others, knowing that you never arrive as a leader and can always learn more.

Conversely, if you're wondering how to help build a kinder culture by caring more, here's a quick tip. Adding a small daily act of kindness, or even just a reminder to bring your most positive self to work, can boost your odds of doing so. Occasionally, all it takes is an extra bullet point on your notepad or a calendar item saying, 'Invite Helen for a coffee to see how she's doing.' Turning a kind intention into a small daily goal prioritises its importance, which will prime your brain to look for an opportunity to deliver on it.

To finish on a positive note, the world is also full of great leaders who get it and understand that they set the tone. We all know the difference they can make to your wellbeing. So, if you have one of those leaders, remember to thank them too. You'll be amazed at how many people take outstanding leadership for granted. And equally, you'll be amazed how many leaders never get genuinely thanked. Remember, too, that very successful people have their mental health challenges, bad habits, gaps in their knowledge, moments of self-doubt, imperfect routines, insecurities and imposter syndrome. Yes, it's true; even the very best leaders have that. A kind word in their direction might make all the difference.

My third tip revolves around language and communication. We all still remember how lonely and isolated we often felt during the pandemic. We generally crave more communication, not less, because communication is a form of connection. Over the years, many managers have asked me whether too much contact with their team will result in that team believing they are not trusted. And I'm always very clear in my answer, which is no. There is a world of difference between a team feeling that the manager is checking up on their work rather than checking in with them as people. The key is to get the tone and the message right and ensure you create time for unstructured conversations just as Sharon, my old boss, did.

It's also important to remember this. One of the most poorly used questions in the English language is 'How are you?' What do I mean by that? I'll answer that with another question: when many people ask that question, are most genuinely interested in the answer? I think not. It has become just something you say as a conversation starter, a convention rather than a real question.

Asked in this way means that probably 99% of people respond with the same superficial answer along the lines of 'ok, thanks' or 'fine'. However, imagine what would happen if, having received a very superficial response, the person asking the question then said, 'No, I mean, how are you really?' and waited intently for the answer. It would have a profound effect on the other person. Asking that simple question in this more intentional and genuine way displays a level of interest and kindness capable of making a difference in almost every conversation you have in the workplace. I call this the power of 'How Are You?' Ask that question twice and you will be amazed at its impact.

One of the biggest clients I've ever worked with discovered this in the starkest terms possible. Their 76,000 employees were asked whether the organisation cared about them. The results were staggering: 50% said not, citing the impact of their line manager as evidence of this. The data gathered also revealed that those line managers who consistently failed to ask about employees' wellbeing before diving into work-related matters were the most significant factor. This insight underscores the critical role of line managers in fostering a supportive work environment and reminds me again of just how empathic Sharon, my old boss, was. Even when time was tight, if you'll remember, she made sure she always checked in with her team at the start of the sales meetings, knowing that their state of mind was as important as the figures they were about to report. I've met many people who feel their line manager is almost as important as their life partner in supporting their wellbeing and we know from research done by Gallup, that managers have the greatest impact on how engaged a team feels. It is said that people don't leave jobs, they leave managers and for any employer who cares about creating a kinder culture, these insights must develop environments where managers are trained to support and nurture those in their care.

When you initiate non-work conversations, amazing things happen. You help foster a sense of connection and belonging among colleagues. It boosts morale and cultivates a supportive atmosphere where individuals feel valued beyond their professional contributions. It also encourages empathy, strengthens relationships and enhances overall job satisfaction.

Acknowledging each other's personal lives makes individuals feel understood and supported, leading to increased resilience and improved productivity. And the very best part of all of this? It costs you nothing and it costs a business nothing. That looks like a phenomenal return on investment to me!

You may be reading this and thinking that I live in a constant state of nirvana and that these things could never happen in real life. As you'd imagine, I don't see it this way and I do understand that, to achieve this, many things must change. Yet, most of the things which would make a real difference are within our gift. And nowhere is this truer than in our ability to share our vulnerability. Through my work, I have seen that this is one of the behaviours that separates the great from the good in 21st century leadership.To show you why and how, I will turn to my friend, mentor and the man who played a very important role in encouraging me to follow my current path - Geoff McDonald.

About seven years ago, I was at the Institute of Directors where Geoff was giving a talk. He is among the most articulate, persuasive and intelligent people I know. He's also one of the most passionate advocates globally for the importance of mental health. When he speaks, people listen and that day was no different. He opened by offering a challenge to the entire room. It is a favourite weapon in Geoff's presentation armoury and it works every time to get people to focus on the topic.

'Most of you don't care about mental health. You're here to tick a box,' he started.

I could feel the room bristle. He then challenged everyone to tell their mental health story when they returned to their office.

'I know what most of you are thinking. You're thinking: I haven't got a mental health story like you. I'm lucky. I've never experienced mental health challenges. So how can I go back to my business and tell my mental health story.'

Geoff then encouraged the audience to look beyond their lives for stories to share, even if they didn't have their own. He described how it could be a sister, an uncle, a best friend or a next-door neighbour.

'Tell the story,' he explained, 'and tell people how it has impacted your life.'

At that moment, Geoff opened people's minds to two critical things. Firstly, the notion that mental health issues can have an impact on all of us and it can be a vast arc. We can be affected by the struggles of people close to us just as much as when we experience issues ourselves. Some of us may feel the suffering of our loved ones much more than our own suffering. Secondly, Geoff opened the audience's eyes to the importance of sharing your vulnerability that day. When you do, you permit others to do the same and this act alone can have the most potent impact imaginable. I've seen it happen so many times with my clients. During a very powerful session I ran with the Royal Navy, I witnessed very senior people share their experiences of struggling with their mental health. In one stroke, it permitted many more people including more junior people to describe their own experiences. Articulating these meant they were able to share these struggles and we all know that an issue shared is an issue halved. From all my work, I'm very clear about one thing. Sharing your vulnerabilities in a way that you feel comfortable will help you enormously, but it will also help your teams to do the same. This helps to foster a culture or environment where the silence around mental health can be broken.

My final thought around communication involves learning how to listen much more mindfully. It is said that we were given two ears and one mouth for a reason: to listen twice as much as we speak. This proportion guides effective communication. Creating kinder cultures is about creating an environment where people can be seen, appreciated and valued for who they are and that takes listening and hearing. Mindful or active listening is an incredibly helpful technique and I'm going to talk more about it later in chapter 13, 'Notice don't interpret'. During conversations with your colleagues, please pay close attention to what they say. Stop mentally planning your response and keep your eyes on the speaker and their nonverbal cues. It takes some practice to develop this skill but running through this same approach as often and with as many people as possible will make all the difference. Are you the kind of person who waits impatiently for someone to finish speaking so that the world can hear your considerable wisdom? Worse still, do you constantly interrupt people? You may need to practice more mindful listening if you recognise either of these traits.

Creating kinder cultures is one of the most important ways we can remove the stigma of mental health in the workplace. An obsession with wellbeing at the top of the leadership team makes a huge difference, as does developing great managers and optimising your language and how you use it. Sadly, in my experience, most organisations are still living in the dark ages when it comes to creating kinder cultures. There is so much more to do.

It is time to create kinder cultures to help break the silence.

Chapter 9
Adults need playtime

I t's that time at school that every child loves. Some call it golden time; others call it free play. Whatever name it's given, it's that glorious hour when children can decide to do whatever interests them the most. During one of these moments, the eight-year-old heroine of this story is enthusiastically drawing because she loves art. She is busy and very excited about what she's creating.

So much so that when the teacher comes over to check on her progress, the child quickly covers up her work.

'What are you doing?' asks the interested teacher.

'I'm drawing, Miss,' replies the child, focusing on colouring in the picture.

'That's lovely; what are you drawing?' the teacher continues.

'I'm drawing God, Miss.'

'That's interesting because no one knows what God looks like,' the teacher points out.

At that moment, the child looks up in bemusement and says, 'They will in a minute.'

I love that story for so many reasons, not least because it demonstrates how beautifully curious and straightforward children often are. It also points to the actual value of play and its role in creativity and wellbeing. But here's the problem. As adults, we often lose sight of the importance of play but, as the title of this chapter suggests, adults desperately need playtime too for reasons I'll explore.

Before I do, though, here's another story that sums up the theme of this chapter beautifully. We are at another school. This time we're in the middle of a school playground. Picture the scene: it's a bright, sunny spring day and the flowers that run along the grassy verge beside the play area have emerged from their winter slumber. The glorious and life-affirming sound of children laughing and playing fills the air as the teachers, who are on playground duty, stand together, chatting and keeping half an eye on naughty Will in the middle of the group. Suddenly, one of the younger children emerges from the group and darts towards a teacher. Still slightly out of breath, she stops and asks a question that leaves the teacher dumbfounded: 'Why don't the teachers come to the playground and play with each other just like we do?'

Silence ensued, followed by a vague explanation about it not happening because of a lack of time. Later that day, however, the teacher explained what had happened to the headteacher. Much laughter ensued followed by a moment's reflection by the head. One thing led to another and a week later, the school implemented a playground role reversal day. Learning support assistants were put in place to supervise the children, letters went out to parents explaining what was happening and the teachers were given a three-line whip. It was time for them to enjoy their playtime in front of the children.

The build-up to that day was fantastic. The children counted the days to the teacher's playtime, excited to witness their fun and games. On the morning in question, children were jostling to seize vantage points around the school, desperate to see which teachers could run the fastest or swing their hips the most to keep the hoop from falling. The event turned out to be the dampest of damp squibs. Why? Because the teachers didn't play at all. They stood around and talked or spent the time with their heads down looking at their phones. The truth was that they had all forgotten how to play or, worse still, felt embarrassed to do so.

Behind this true story of an enlightened and experimental head and a bunch of teachers who'd forgotten the joy of play, lies a very serious point about our wellbeing. Why do schools allow children to have a break during the day? Almost every teacher I know would say it's down to four reasons. It's a break between two pieces of work. If you want them to go from geography to English, it serves as a chance to re-energise them. Secondly, getting them outside means they're in the fresh air and, hopefully, sunshine and we all know the impact that has. Crucially, it's fun to be with your mates so the third reason is the opportunity for social interaction and a chance to laugh, chat and play games. Finally, it's a chance to stretch your legs, run around the playground and get some exercise. Now, let's relate this issue of play to the working environment.

Going from geography to English is like rushing from one client call to another. The exercise from running around the playground is vital to a child's wellbeing as is getting fresh air into their lungs; two things just as important for adults but made more challenging by working from home. Having fun with your mates in the playground is the same as engaging with each other in a playful way at work. You see where I'm going with this. If you still don't believe me, look at the work of Dr Stuart Brown, a psychiatrist and researcher, who has extensively studied the importance of play in human development and wellbeing. He founded the National Institute for Play, an organisation dedicated to advancing the understanding of play and its significance in our lives. His work has focused on children and adults, emphasising that play is not just a childhood activity but a vital component of a healthy and fulfilling life at any age. Through his research, he has explored how play influences creativity, problem-solving, stress reduction and overall mental health in individuals. Let's look at three of these in a bit more detail.

Dr Brown's research demonstrates that play can significantly boost creativity and innovation in adults. He notes that when adults engage in playful activities, they stimulate their imagination and explore new possibilities. For example, when people participate in creative hobbies like painting, sculpting or playing musical instruments purely for enjoyment, they often discover new ideas and innovative approaches to problem-solving. Playful exploration allows adults to think outside the box and come up with fresh solutions to the challenges they encounter in their professional lives. And how many organisations do you know that don't want to solve problems? Of course, the answer is none, so why isn't play at the heart of every organisation's strategy?

Playtime is a powerful stress reliever for adults. Dr Brown's research suggests that play triggers the release of endorphins, the body's natural mood elevators, which counteract stress hormones like cortisol. Engaging in activities such as sports or outdoor adventures allows adults to momentarily escape the pressures of everyday life, reduce anxiety and promote emotional wellbeing. Dr Brown has shown that regular play can contribute to lower stress levels and decreased symptoms of depression. So again, why don't more companies reflect this in what they do? If I were running a big company today, I'd ban sitting down to lunch with partners or clients and institute a walking lunch policy. Get a sandwich for the person or people you're meeting, head to the nearest convenient green space and walk and talk for an hour. You could even head to the swings for 10 minutes if you're feeling adventurous! This kind of lunch meeting is cheaper and healthier and you'll develop more innovative ways of improving your relationships with your clients.

Finally, play fosters social interaction and strengthens interpersonal relationships among adults. Dr Brown emphasises that participating in playful activities with colleagues can create a sense of camaraderie and trust. The social connections formed through play enhance our quality of life and support us during challenging times and build stronger, more resilient relationships.

All the research I've read also underscores that adults prioritising play tend to have better and more fulfilling social networks. So, why don't more organisations nurture this camaraderie and trust? Well, because they still need to grasp the critical importance of play. Rather than see it as a frivolous activity, play must be seen as a necessity and a vital part of any organisation's strategy.

One final virtual high five to the work of Dr Brown. I love the title of one of his books on this subject; 'Play: how it shapes the brain, opens the imagination and invigorates the soul'. The brain, the imagination and the soul. All three helped by acknowledging the importance of play and all three vital to wellbeing. In many ways, my work revolves around a battle for the soul of most organisations. Suppose a kinder culture doesn't exist and people are not revered as an organisation's greatest asset. There is no room for play here. Of course, those organisations are the ones whose CEO might read this chapter and think I am as mad as a box of frogs (and there will be more of frogs in the next chapter). That mythical CEO would be wrong because, even if they didn't believe me or Dr Stuart Brown, I'd ask them to consider this:

Why do some of the most successful companies on the planet use the value of play to drive real shareholder value?

Why do Google campuses worldwide include recreational spaces with relaxation zones where employees can take short breaks?

Do you think Apple is barking mad because it encourages its employees to participate in brainstorming sessions that often involve play such as building prototypes with LEGO or using design thinking techniques to solve complex problems?

Do you question the sanity of Pixar's CEO? Their feedback process, in which team members sit in a circle and playfully brainstorm, acting out scenes and engaging in creative discussions, often using toys and props?

Finally, why have companies like Slack found creative ways to integrate play into the workplace in an age of remote work and virtual offices? They have a dedicated water cooler channel where employees can share jokes, memes and content that has nothing to do with work. The answer to those questions is obvious: around £5 trillion.

That's the rough value of those four businesses combined. So, any CEO claiming that playtime isn't a commercial imperative must take a long, hard look at themselves. I know this, too, from my own experience during the pandemic. So many of the things that constituted my playtime were taken away; my beloved Watford FC, chatting to my mates in the pub and chasing a squash ball around a court. All these things help me achieve the right balance in life. Without them, I was amazed at how off kilter my life became and the difference that made to how I regularly felt.

That balance between work and play is crucial for our overall wellbeing and productivity. In academic terms, it's not just Dr Brown who shows us the way. A study by the University of Pennsylvania's Wharton School of Business found that employees who engage in leisure activities outside work are happier and more productive. The researchers discovered that individuals who make time for leisure pursuits such as hobbies, sports or spending time with loved ones are better able to recharge and maintain a healthy work-life balance. As a result, they exhibit higher levels of job performance and are more resilient in workplace challenges.

Adults need playtime. It brings balance and embracing the importance of balance empowers them to lead healthier, more enriched lives. Doing this is one of the most important ways to look after our mental health, both in and out of work.

Let's prioritise playtime to help break the silence.

Chapter 10
Don't be a frog

There are nearly 5,000 species of frogs in the world today and they are remarkable little creatures. The nature of their skin allows them to breathe through it, making them highly adaptable to water and land. They play a vital role in controlling insect populations, helping to keep pest populations in check. They also shed light on evolution, embryology and medical advances.

Their remarkable ability to regenerate lost body parts holds potential for human regenerative medicine. I could go on, but you didn't buy this book for a lesson in the natural world and I'm certainly no Sir David Attenborough. So why this chapter title and what do frogs have to do with mental health?

They say that if you drop a frog into boiling water (not something I'd ever suggest), the shock of the temperature will allow its instinct to take over. It will find a way out of that pot faster than you'd lose a toupee in a hurricane. On the other hand, if you drop a frog into a pot of tepid water and place that pot on low heat and gradually bring it to the boil (again, not something I'd suggest doing), the frog will be oblivious to the rising temperature and eventually perish in the boiling water.

Whenever I recount that story, I always wait nervously for someone better informed than I am to shoot it down. I remember once addressing a room full of research scientists, doctors and highly academic people. As soon as I mentioned the frog story, I couldn't help but notice the tell-tale glow of smartphone screens as people began to google it. Occasionally, in sessions like that, someone kindly interjects, 'I hate to burst your bubble, David, but apparently...'

So, it's important to clarify that this story is grounded in something other than rigorous scientific research on frog behaviour. But, as I know from many years in the advertising world, there are times when you shouldn't let the truth stand in the way of a good story. Whether factually accurate or not, this story has a significant place in my work because it's a powerful metaphor for the way we overlook the gradual deterioration of our mental health.

This process is also the way we live our lives. We adapt to stress, anxiety and life's challenges over time. We may not notice the gradual increase in pressure until we're at boiling point. Just as the frog perceives the warming water as comfortable, we might initially perceive stress or a high-pressure lifestyle as normal. We convince ourselves it's part of the daily grind and something we can handle. This normalisation can be dangerous because it prevents us from recognising that we're in danger of burnout. Of course, frogs don't possess the cognitive ability to self-reflect and identify changes in their environment.

Similarly, many of us lack self-awareness when it comes to our mental health. We might ignore signs of anxiety or depression, attributing them to external factors or brushing them off as temporary stress. Finally, just as the frog initially adapts to the warming water, we often try to cope with mounting stress by soldiering on. The world we live in frequently pressures us to do just that. We might think 'I've handled worse before' or 'I'll tough it out'. This resilience can sometimes be good but, when taken to extremes, it prevents us from seeking the help we need.

To further illustrate this broader point, let's consider our behaviour and the evidence relating to how we respond to physical and mental challenges. In an earlier chapter, I mentioned the absurd notion that you wouldn't stop going to the doctor completely just because you had encountered one you weren't sure about. Yet, in my work, I meet so many people who, because of one tricky experience with a counsellor, decide that counselling isn't for them. I do understand why this is. The problem lies in the need for more information and transparency. When referred to a counsellor like me, you rarely know or have explained to you the various therapeutic modalities available and how they might help you. Few counsellors take the time to explain their approach at the beginning of the relationship. So, we end up in counselling without a clear understanding of what to expect. It's like going into a doctor's office without knowing what they do or what to expect when you sit opposite them. Or worse still, what impact their advice will have.

But how do we respond to our physical and emotional needs? The answer is in very different ways. If we have a chronic stomach ache or significant pain somewhere, the evidence is that we will usually contact our GP within 24 to 48 hours. Yet, if we are feeling off-colour mentally or beginning to show signs of burnout, how long, on average, do you think it takes for us to seek help and talk to someone? A week? A month? A year? Unbelievably, it's an average of seven years before we decide to seek help with our mental health. I don't need to tell you that, quite often, that's too late. Every week, on average, 115 people die through suicide which is one of the many reasons why my life's work is now to help people break their silence. The core message here is clear: we act swiftly regarding our physical health. If we break a leg, the pain forces us into immediate action. We rush to the hospital without a second thought. However, when it comes to our mental health, it's a whole different and potentially fatal approach.

Like the frog, we don't know we are slowly cooking. That's why our ability to notice change in ourselves and others matters. I began to look at this in chapter five, 'Can you measure your mental health?' with the story of Gary whose subjective wellbeing score dropped from a 10 to a nine but whose mental distress we missed because we all assumed that a nine was fine. Unlike Sharon who looked for variation as a sign that something might be wrong, we didn't think about the fact that his score had dropped. Later in the book, I will explore further why it's essential to notice, but not interpret change, and why noticing change is critical. But for now, please understand that it's the change that matters: changes in your sleep patterns, your ability to stay focused, lesser enjoyment of the things you love doing or a general decline in your energy levels.

Occasionally, experiencing some of these symptoms is perfectly normal: life is tough and we all have ups and downs. But, if these symptoms persist over an extended period, it's a signal to seek professional help. And, of course, it's not just about paying attention to the changes you might personally experience. We must all look out for and look after each other because it's almost impossible to know who might be struggling in our immediate circle of close friends, family and colleagues. I suspect some people reading this book grew up in a world where you assumed everyone was ok. I wonder how supportive we'd be of each other if we thought that no one was fine and that everyone needed support. It's a mindset shift and I'm not advocating for an overly protective approach to people. I'm simply suggesting that we might all need to shift our approach from one that sometimes borders on apathy or indifference to one that actively seeks to understand how someone is feeling. How many times have we all read heart-breaking stories of people who have lost loved ones to suicide and heard them wish that they had noticed more, talked more and assumed less? The silence I keep referring to is created by the stigma around mental health, but it's also fuelled by the assumption that those around us are probably ok and that we don't actively need to check in with them. If we want to break the silence, then it shouldn't just be the responsibility of those suffering to speak out; we should all be actively looking to break that silence by asking 'how are you?' for the second time and really listening to the answer.

As I've observed in this book, what we pay attention to grows. It's so true, and I want to give you some practical advice on how to avoid becoming our metaphorical frog. How can you notice those changes, which might seem small in isolation but, as we've highlighted already, can add up to something much more destructive over time? Here are a few tips you might find useful:

Why not keep a sleep diary? Record your bedtime, wake-up time and any disturbances during the night for at least a week. If you look for patterns of irregularities such as difficulty falling asleep, regularly waking up, difficulty going back to sleep or waking up very early, you might want to be less frog and to think about the temperature of the water around you. You could also track the number of hours you sleep each night. A noticeable decrease in the amount of sleep you get might mean that the water in the pot is simmering. Pay attention to whether you feel exhausted during the day and monitor your ability to concentrate on tasks by noticing how long you can stay focused without becoming distracted. Any significant decrease in your concentration span could indicate a rising temperature. Very often, when we feel anxious or flat, we find it hard to get things done. Try to note the number of tasks you complete within a specific timeframe. If you struggle to finish previously manageable tasks, you may need to reflect on why. Try to add the following things to your list of good mental health measures.

Take notice of the frequency and types of distractions that disrupt your work or play and try to recognise if the distractions have become more frequent. Pay attention to your interactions with friends and family. It could be something to watch if you withdraw from social activities or feel less enthusiastic about spending time with loved ones. And finally, be alive to your hobbies and interests. A drop in enthusiasm or engagement is a sure sign to look out for. After doing things you love, rate your enjoyment from one to 10.

Remember what I mentioned earlier in the book? We don't treasure what we can't measure, so rating things like this is essential. Compare these ratings over time and notice whether you consistently rate activities lower. I know people who write down their scores and find it helpful to reflect on any changes, so I know it works. I also know people who rate their energy levels on a scale from one to 10 at various points throughout the day because they want to notice consistently low scores.

This process also helps you to notice symptoms like fatigue, weakness, or lethargy. I'd be amazed if this was new news to you but do monitor your caffeine and sugar intake. Changes in your energy levels can be influenced by diet. Keep track of how much caffeine and sugary foods and drinks you have.

We all know that excessive intake can lead to energy fluctuations, which are not helpful for our mental health.

This list is not exhaustive and certainly not intended as a self-help guide to improving these areas of your life. They serve as a reminder that you must pay attention first and foremost before taking whatever action you feel is essential. Now, at this stage, you may be thinking, 'Hang on a minute Beeney, I don't have time for all this. I've got a job, a family and a thousand things on my to-do list.' Everyone's mental health is unique and everyone will have their ways of monitoring and supporting themselves and others. I'm not suggesting that the list above should be a daily routine. It's a series of suggestions that I've discovered, from the work I've done for myself and my clients, to be a useful way of noticing what's going on. Take from it what you think will help in the knowledge that, for most people, the water warms up at times in their lives. You must look out for the changes that serve as a red flag for how you might be feeling. Without a strategy for recognising the changes in temperature around you, you might eventually be boiled alive.

It is time to take notice so you can break the silence.

Chapter 11
A can of worms

It's a tangled web, a slippery slope, a delicate matter or a knotty problem. The more literary-minded leaders have told me it's a Pandora's box. There are even those who describe it as a can of worms. I am, of course, talking about the language some leaders use to refer to the subject of mental health. In many ways, a can of worms is a helpful metaphor. If you think of the can as the company and the worms wriggling around inside as the many issues impacting the mental health of its employees, it's little wonder that some people don't want to open the can. In this chapter, though, that's precisely what we will do.

I cherish my work, but it also brings me down at times. I start my presentations with a slide which reads 'Creating kinder cultures' and there have been many times when I have been asked to remove the word 'kinder' by the leader organising the session because there is a concern that it's too fluffy and not business-minded enough. That lack of understanding of the power of kindness and the fundamental need to change workplace culture leaves me feeling low-spirited and pessimistic. It's the same feeling when senior leaders have neither the interest, nor the good everyday leadership sense to show up and participate in the workshop. Or, worse still, those times when leaders want me to be there as a box-ticking exercise because their HR department have told them it must be part of the organisation's training programme. All these moments are the most unambiguous indication that the stigma of mental health is ever-present, yet the problem is not considered serious. Those organisations that place little or no value on mental health are, very sadly, still in the majority.

As I've said every day for the last eight years, businesses that create kinder cultures will optimise the performance of their people, be more productive and succeed faster. Mental health in the workplace is a far from fluffy subject. Looking after people is vital because they are integral to long-term growth.

Failure to embrace this results in higher staff churn, more colleagues on long-term sick leave and people operating on low energy. In March 2022, Deloitte published new mental health research revealing that the cost to employers of poor mental health had increased from £45 billion in 2019 to £56 billion in 2021. The pandemic influenced that increase, but taking the 2019 number alone, I'd argue that this number represents £45 billion of wasted human capital because of poor leadership and an inability to understand the issue of mental health in the workplace.

The big question is, what do we do about this and what action is required to stem the tide of apathy around mental health? As you now know, this is my life's work but for my mission to succeed, it requires leaders to understand what might be inside that can of worms and how to empty it. It requires them to have the courage, energy and insight to open the can regardless of how difficult that might seem and create a culture where silence isn't the norm. It also requires employees to break the silence and call out the behaviours that build toxic cultures. Over the years, I've noticed plenty of these behaviours and, more importantly, heard first-hand about them from the teams I engage with. So, if you're a leader, I'm about to shine a powerful magnifying glass on what I know you should be doing to create a kinder culture. Equally, if you work as part of a team, get a pen and paper and prepare to make notes for your next chat with the person who leads your team. It's important to say that I'm neither a leadership coach nor an expert in the issues facing leaders, but I have seen enough examples of leadership through my work to make highly informed judgements. All I'm keen to do is point out the many problems I've encountered over the years, knowing that they represent the red flags to be aware of in working environments that stigmatise mental health.

We all know that communication is the lifeblood of outstanding leadership. It's the glue that binds leaders to their teams and organisations. When leaders transparently share their vision, goals, and challenges, it builds trust. Trust, in turn, leads to increased loyalty and commitment. Communication also makes sure that everyone is pointing in the same direction. The best leader ensures that every colleague understands the organisation's objectives and everyone's role in those objectives. Crucially, in the context of this book, communication leads to greater employee motivation which, in turn, helps morale. When leaders tell their teams how grateful they are for all their efforts, it boosts morale and motivates team members to give their best.

From my career, I know that being valued, supported and encouraged by my team leaders has significantly impacted my wellbeing in a positive way. During those times in my career when that hasn't happened, I've gone into my shell and been less open around my boss because I've felt more intimidated. Open communication channels in any organisation allow leaders to be aware of issues and conflicts early on, ensuring things can be resolved quickly and kindly. Communication matters and it's almost certain that those who don't place it at the very heart of leadership will not engage in open and honest conversations about mental health issues or actively listen to their employees' concerns. They are the leaders who want to keep this kind of worm firmly inside the can.

I have never liked the phrase 'work-life balance'. It doesn't represent how most of us think about the relationship between those two things. We have one life and our work is simply part of that life. If you're an employer, your responsibility is to make this part of your team's life, which is work, as meaningful as possible. It's why the leader who consistently allows long hours to happen and who expects employees to prioritise work over their personal lives is harmful in our collective battle to remove the stigma of mental health in the workplace. I'm not saying for one moment that companies don't deserve or need total team commitment. They do, but unrealistic expectations from leaders regarding what their teams should contribute is another major red flag.

Casual racism is corrosive. It erodes the very foundations of our society and, of course, it is to be despised. It thrives on stereotypes, biases and discriminatory attitudes that persist beneath the surface. We've seen it perpetuate division and inequality. It can often manifest as offhand remarks, microaggressions or jokes but its impact is profound and devastating. Why do I even mention this? Well, because those offhand remarks, microaggressions and jokes are the ones replicated in the workplace when it comes to the subject of mental health. You know the ones I mean. The observation that 'you're being too sensitive' immediately ensuring that individuals feel invalidated and unable to express their emotions or concerns. Or what about 'just toughen up', implying someone should suppress their feelings, stop being so fragile and not ask for help? What is the impact of telling someone that they are always too negative or to stop overthinking? It stigmatises people's emotional responses and trivialises significant thought processes. And finally, perhaps the phrase that should have you reviewing your life options fastest of all. 'This job is not for the faint of heart.' There is no more unmistakable sign that your boss might be building a culture glorifying overwork, stress and burnout. So, just like the casual racist, beware the casual 'mental healthist'. I think I may have just made that phrase up but, in this context, it works. Beware offhand remarks, attempts to belittle and supposed jokes about your feelings. They all signify something more pernicious and you should avoid being around them like the plague.

Next up in the leadership gallery of shame around mental health, or other worms in that can we're now examining, is micromanaging. We've all seen it and we all know its profoundly negative impact on mental health. Do you work in an environment where your every move is scrutinised and you're constantly second-guessed? It's like trying to walk on eggshells and is incredibly stressful. Micromanagement undermines confidence. When someone is always looking over your shoulder, it sends the message that you're not trusted to do your job competently. This management style erodes self-esteem and can lead to self-doubt. It also generates anxiety. The constant pressure to meet someone else's exacting standards and the fear of making mistakes can lead to heightened stress levels. This chronic stress can have long-term health consequences. Micromanagement means longer hours at work as you struggle to meet all the demands placed on you. And we all know what longer hours do. In the end, being micromanaged is like carrying a heavy backpack of stress and frustration and, over time, it can take a severe toll on mental health. It's also a guaranteed sign that you're living in a professional world that doesn't want to get anywhere near breaking the silence.

Another of the worms wriggling inside our can is the one that penalises employees for taking sick days or mental health days, sending a clear and damaging message that taking care of your health and wellbeing is not valued. It creates a culture of fear and anxiety because it discourages transparency. When employees fear consequences for taking time off, they're more likely to come to work when they should be resting or seeking help and hiding their illnesses or struggles. It perpetuates presenteeism so that employees show up for work despite being unwell, leading to decreased productivity, lower-quality work and the potential for longer recovery times. In the long run, a culture that penalises employees for taking sick or mental health days creates a less healthy, less engaged and less loyal workforce. Most importantly, it means that the stigma of mental health in the workplace is alive and kicking.

Overseeing a culture of favoured employees is a guaranteed way to create a toxic environment that erodes trust, damages morale and harms team cohesion. When employees witness their colleagues receiving special treatment, whether in terms of promotions, leniency or access to resources, it breeds feelings of unfairness and injustice. This can lead to intense resentment, as those left feeling overlooked or undervalued experience heightened stress and frustration. Neglecting the mental health needs of some while providing support to others deepens this division. If, for example, one employee is granted time off for mental health reasons while another is denied or faces repercussions, it sends a clear message that the organisation doesn't prioritise the wellbeing of all its employees equally. This issue not only creates a sense of exclusion but can also exacerbate mental health issues among those who feel overlooked. Ultimately, favouritism and neglect of mental health drive a wedge within the team, hindering collaboration, creativity and overall productivity. Organisations must cultivate a fair culture and prioritise all employees' wellbeing equally to foster a healthier and more harmonious work environment. When employees know they are valued and treated fairly, they are more likely to work together effectively and support one another's mental health needs. If that doesn't happen, it's all the evidence you need that yours is a working environment that doesn't want to nurture a culture in which wellbeing is high on the leadership agenda.

So, and for the final time, back to our can of worms. It's a helpful way to examine why leaders neglect mental health. It also vividly explains why they want to suppress many of the issues, hoping these magically disappear. What they fail to grasp, though, is that the can of worms is of their own making. Those subterranean wrigglers are the evidence you need to spot an organisation that is highly likely to perpetuate the stigma of mental health, so it's no wonder that some leaders don't want to open the can. Breaking the silence is the only way we will make change happen. If you're an employee and see these worms contracting and undulating as they make their way through the company, call it out and explain why. If you're a leader and any of these worms look familiar to you, it's time to do something about them. If you are prepared to open that can and eliminate them, you'll have a happier, healthier and more productive workforce.

It is time to break the silence.

Chapter 12
Lower your bar

Watford lift the FA Cup for the first time. If I ever were to read them, these nine words would mean I'd just lived through one of the happiest days of my life. I've no idea if I'll ever see those words in my lifetime - probably not, in truth - but there are nine other words that I never imagined I'd read either. These nine words have allowed me to truly understand how to lower your bar to improve your wellbeing and performance (and I'll describe what I mean by lowering your bar in a moment). The nine words are:

My panic attacks have become a blessing in disguise.

Given how I described the impact of my panic attacks at the start of this book, these words might seem rather strange. However, let me explain what I mean by this. One of the questions I'm most frequently asked in my work is about my panic attacks.

When people understand that I suffer from them, they are always interested to know when they happen and how often. But before I answer that question, I always deal with the question I suspect people are probably more interested in but, understandably, too afraid to ask. What would happen if I had a panic attack while presenting? It's an important thing to ask because, since starting my business, I've done thousands of presentations to some of the world's most significant and impressive organisations. To be clear, that's not me blowing my own trumpet. I make that point only to suggest that all the conditions you'd expect to come into play to cause my panic attacks are often present in my work. Lots of people, some of whom are very senior, an emotionally charged subject and hundreds of pairs of eyes bearing down on me like metaphorical lasers. And, of course, added to that, it's just me. I'm the only one delivering the presentation so I've nowhere to hide. When you think back to the panic attacks I shared with you at the start of this book, I wouldn't be surprised if you were also wondering what happens if I have one while I'm presenting. However, I have managed to get through almost every talk and presentation over the past eight years without having a panic attack, despite the daily worry about the possibility of having one. If you cast your mind back to some of the earliest chapters in the book, you'll remember that I certainly didn't escape those types of demons in my corporate career, so what's changed? The answer lies at the heart of my journey towards understanding self-compassion, which revolves around genuinely embracing three things. First, an acceptance that it's ok not to be ok. It's a well-used phrase today in mental health but there's a good reason it's used so widely. It speaks to a universal truth that recognises that we all face moments of vulnerability and hardship and that these moments are the very times that we should seek out other people for support.

There's a second reason that I'm able to overcome my panic attacks when it matters most and it's something I've talked about already in the book. It's so crucial to this book's overall theme that I will reiterate it. You can also tell how important it is because there's an entire chapter on the subject before you get to the end of this book. Suffice it to say, I genuinely believe that you inspire people when you share vulnerability. I talked about this earlier in chapter eight, 'Creating kinder cultures', when I referenced witnessing the powerful effect of a leader or a senior person in an organisation being open and vulnerable. When I'm talking about my vulnerabilities, knowing that I'm helping others share theirs helps me enormously.

But the demons are still hanging around before every one of my talks. I still find myself hearing their voices and battling them in my head. When I first meet people, I'm always smiling and laughing. What they're not aware of is what's going on inside my head as I'm thinking, 'Oh, please don't have a panic attack today.' But one of the reasons those voices are less powerful now is because of something that occurred to me some time ago—a counter-intuitive thought that lifted a heavy weight from my shoulders: Does it matter if I have a panic attack in front of everyone? Of course, the answer is no. If I do, I said to myself, let them see what a panic attack feels like for me.

I can talk them through it and explain what's going on as I become breathless.

The magical thing was that, from the moment I permitted myself to have a panic attack, I reduced the chances of it happening because I wasn't fighting it anymore. I discovered that if I lowered my bar, took away the fear of having a panic attack and reduced the pressure on myself, my sessions became more dynamic, informative and engaging. I could feel it almost immediately and it transformed my relationship with my work and my panic attacks. They had become that blessing in disguise I was talking about earlier. Of course, they never go away and possibly never will but lowering that bar has profoundly affected my day-to-day life. Permitting myself to have a panic attack and being much kinder to myself in the process has radically reduced the chances of them happening.

Could lowering the bar help you? Can you find ways to do that and feel better? Like many aspects of this book, my stories and the story of my journey are only half the reason I've written it. The other half is to act as a guide and a prompt to help you find your means to break the silence. Here are a few ways I've seen people successfully lower their bar.

Let's start with something important but often overlooked and something I referenced earlier in chapter seven, 'One in one': the importance of being kind to yourself. Imagine having your own personal cheerleader right there with you, ready to give you a pep talk and support you when things get tough at work. That's what self-compassion is all about in the workplace. Instead of being hard on yourself when you mess up or face setbacks, treat yourself with the same kindness you'd show to a friend or co-worker. Why should you treat yourself any differently? You should probably be even kinder to yourself than you are to others. Lots of research shows that self-compassion can boost your resilience and motivation. You can start building self-compassion by reflecting on your feelings, being empathic towards yourself and giving yourself positive affirmations. When you encounter challenges or make mistakes at work, acknowledge your emotions, remind yourself that it's perfectly ok to make mistakes and focus on what you can learn and how you can grow from the experience. This also helps cultivate the growth mindset I talked about in that same chapter. Shifting your perspective like this can help you be less critical of yourself and create a healthier environment within you, ultimately helping you achieve more.

I'm a big fan of the concept of the growth mindset which I described earlier in the book. Hard work and dedication can improve our abilities and intelligence. This mindset can seriously change things at work.Instead of shooting for the stars and expecting instant success, a growth mindset is about learning and trying something out. When you run into challenges or things don't go as planned, see them as opportunities to grow, not as failures to achieve. By doing this, you're not just letting go of the perfectionist in you but also building up your resilience and creativity. That way, you can achieve even more in the long run. A common trap many people fall into at work is setting ambitious goals that make them feel like they're constantly playing catch-up. It's better to go easy on yourself. That means setting goals that make sense and patting yourself on the back for even the little wins. Start by breaking those significant objectives into smaller, more manageable tasks. It makes the goals less scary and gives you plenty of chances to feel you've accomplished something. And don't be shy about celebrating those victories – they all add to your overall progress, no matter how small they seem. Recognising your progress boosts your self-esteem and motivation, helping you keep going and achieve more sustainably and compassionately.

Many of us feel the burden at work of doing it all ourselves. We're afraid that asking for help or delegating tasks makes us look weak or not up to the job. However, delegating is a critical skill for personal and professional growth. It's not about being lazy or incapable; it's about being intelligent and strategic. When you pass on specific tasks to your colleagues, you free up your time and brainpower to focus on where you can shine. This process lightens your workload, encourages teamwork and helps your colleagues grow. Remember, lowering the bar in some areas can help you excel in many others.

Finally, here's an idea that works well for people who become fixed on the thought that the ones who concentrate longest win. That just isn't true. Here's an interesting concept to boost your performance at work – it's called 'micro-sprints'. Instead of aiming for long, uninterrupted work hours, try breaking your day into shorter, highly focused work intervals. These could be as short as 20-30 minutes. During these micro-sprints, your sole focus is on a specific task or project. You must avoid distractions and multitasking – just laser-like concentration for a short time. After each micro-sprint, take a quick break to recharge, maybe for just five minutes. Then, dive back into another focused sprint. This approach capitalises on the brain's ability to maintain high concentration levels for shorter periods. It helps you avoid burnout and mental fatigue while accomplishing more in less time. Or in other words, it helps to lower the bar so that you achieve more.

Understanding the benefits of lowering the bar is vital for organisations as well. In fast-paced and demanding work environments, employees often face immense pressure to consistently perform at high levels, leading to stress, burnout and significant mental health issues. Just as we can set unrealistic goals for ourselves, organisations can do the same for their employees. Employers can create a healthier, more sustainable work culture that promotes overall wellbeing by adopting a more flexible and compassionate approach to expectations. In doing this, they bring down levels of anxiety and allow their people to have greater levels of clarity which, in turn, leads to better long-term performance. That idea of performance over the longer term is why lowering expectations never equates to lowering standards or compromising excellence. Instead, it involves setting realistic and meaningful goals considering employees' needs and circumstances. By focusing on continuous improvement and personal growth rather than some false sense of perfection, employers can create a culture of resilience and adaptability that enables employees to thrive in the face of challenges and build long-term value for the organisation. Constantly setting the highest organisational bar which then leads to short-term employee burnout is not a strategy for long-term sustainable growth. It's a strategy designed to kill off the workforce.

So, through the lens of Watford never winning the FA Cup, my panic attacks, self-compassion, a growth mindset and some thoughts about lowering bars, I hope this chapter has given you something to think about, use or pass on. Above all, I hope it's given you a sense that lowering your bar might be the best thing you could do for yourself, not just for how you feel but also for what you achieve. Lowering that bar can come in all shapes and sizes and will require some thinking to ensure you do what works best for you. Whatever that is, it will help you; you might even discover things about yourself that you never knew existed.

It is time to lower the bar to help break the silence.

Chapter 13
Notice, don't interpret

It could be a mate you see less of these days. Or a colleague at work who has become more agitated, frustrated or short-tempered. Your boss might show intense mood swings, ranging from despair to anger or irritability. It's that person you've built a friendship with because you always see each other on the same bus at the same time, but they seem to have lost or gained lots of weight and just don't seem themselves anymore. It's the corridor conversation with the person from another department or part of the business, but they have become more pessimistic and self-critical. And finally, it's the person you're closest to in the world telling you they think they might be a burden. These are all examples of the things that are important to notice when thinking about other people's wellbeing. The critical word in that sentence is notice because understanding the power of noticing rather than interpreting when dealing with other people is crucial and the topic for this chapter.

Some time ago, a friend talked to me about his concerns regarding his daughter's behaviour after meals. Unbeknownst to me, she had been diagnosed with an eating disorder during her teens. He and his wife were deeply worried about her, spending hours watching her but unsure how to approach the situation, fearing they might say the wrong thing. They asked me what they should do. I suggested a simple yet heartfelt approach: they should sit with her and tell her how much they love her. I told them to ensure that part of that conversation involved inquiring about her wellbeing. Very specifically, I said to them that they needed to acknowledge what they had noticed, which was her disappearance after meals, and to ask if everything was ok. It was no more than that. My friend's mood immediately lifted once he realised how much easier that approach was and how much more open a conversation it might lead to. We tend to overthink when it comes to mental health concerns. Instead, we should strive to be more attuned and willing to ask questions, just as we would with physical health issues. Let's examine more closely why noticing is vitally important, how it differs from interpreting and how you can apply this critical skill, just as my friend did, to become a more empathetic and supportive friend, family member or work colleague.

Before diving into the importance of noticing, it's worth looking at what we mean by interpretation. It's a question I'm often asked to expand on in my sessions. Interpretation, in this context, means making assumptions or drawing conclusions about someone's mental state based on their behaviour, words or expressions. It often involves analysing their actions through our own experiences and beliefs. Interpreting this way can cause problems because it relies heavily on our biases, limited understanding and preconceived notions. When we analyse someone's behaviour, we may inadvertently jump to the wrong conclusions, misjudge their emotions or mistake their actions for things we think might be true. Here's a hypothetical but very typical example of what I mean.

Your friend has been quieter than usual lately and they have politely declined your invitation to get together. Their explanation about not meeting up and the indication as to when they might see you next seems sketchy and vague. You might interpret this behaviour as a sign that they are upset with you or no longer value your friendship. The truth is that it may not have anything to do with you. You've interpreted their behaviour through your lens, not theirs. They might be struggling with personal issues unrelated to your friendship or worrying about something in their life that you're not aware of. Interpreting what you think might be the issue can lead to misunderstandings, strained relationships and missed opportunities for support. From the summer of 2017, my dear friend Sue Williams became less and less communicative with me. I convinced myself that I had done something to upset her. In early 2018, Sue took her own life. The regret I feel for assuming Sue's silence was all about my actions will live with me forever. I was projecting my narrative onto hers, which meant I lost the chance to put an arm around her shoulder. Could I have prevented Sue's death? I'll never know, but I do know one thing. I will never make that mistake again.

Now, let's shift our focus to noticing – a skill that involves keen observation and active listening without immediately jumping to conclusions. When you notice, you pay attention to the details of someone's behaviour, emotions and words, allowing them to express themselves without judgements or assumptions. Noticing requires empathy, patience and a willingness to be present in the moment. It means suspending your judgement and avoiding the urge to provide quick fixes or solutions. Instead, you create a safe space for the other person to be open and share their feelings on their terms. By their terms, I mean when they are ready to talk and how much they want to share. When you notice, you might observe subtle changes in a person, such as changes in posture, facial expressions or tone of voice. You listen actively, not just to their words but also trying to hear the emotions beneath them. You ask open-ended questions to encourage them to express themselves without feeling pressured or judged.

Understanding the importance of noticing becomes even more critical when considering this book's central theme. Mental health struggles are often complex and multifaceted and they can show up in various ways. People experiencing mental health issues may not always openly discuss their challenges or ask for help. As we know all too well by now, they might go to great lengths to hide their struggles due to stigma, shame or fear of judgement. In these situations, noticing becomes a lifeline. By observing changes in behaviour, you can recognise when someone might be going through a difficult time, even when they don't explicitly mention it. This early recognition can be instrumental in providing the proper support at the right time.

Noticing also plays a crucial role in combating the stigma surrounding mental health. Stigma arises from misconceptions and judgments about mental health challenges. When we notice rather than interpret, we create a kind, compassionate and understanding environment where people feel safe sharing their experiences. It's worth highlighting here the relationship between creating kinder cultures and the power of noticing. In the end, so many mental health roads lead to the importance of kindness. Imagine that magical workplace I wrote about earlier where employees notice each other's wellbeing, genuinely ask how their colleagues are doing and listen without judgement when someone is open about their mental health. In such an environment, individuals are more likely to seek help when needed, reducing the stigma around mental health and promoting a culture where wellbeing is nurtured. You can see what a vital virtuous circle this is.

Now that we've explored why noticing is crucial, let's look at how you can develop and cultivate this valuable skill. When someone speaks, truly listen to what they are saying. I talked earlier about mindful or active listening in the chapter about creating kinder cultures and this kind of listening is a key part of the process of noticing. Avoid thinking about your response while they're talking and resist the urge to interrupt. Instead, focus on understanding their perspective and really hear what they are saying. Encourage the person to share their thoughts and feelings by asking open-ended questions. 'How have you been feeling lately?' is a good example. These questions invite deeper and more meaningful conversations. Remind yourself not to jump to conclusions or make assumptions. Everyone's experiences are unique and respecting their journey is essential.

Let the person know you're there for them and willing to provide support however they need it and the question 'What do you need?' or 'What can I do to support you?' can be very helpful. Sometimes, someone needs only a listening ear or a shoulder to lean on. Finally, but importantly, just as you are already doing by reading this book, take the time to learn about mental health and the everyday challenges people may face. This knowledge can help you better understand and support those around you. The more knowledge and awareness you have, the more significant the difference you can make.

Always remember that it can be very hard for people to talk about their feelings or share things about themselves that they consider very private. I'll never forget a moment when this issue was brought home to me during my counselling training. Our trainer asked us to write something we would likely take to our grave. That piece of information or feeling that perhaps you've never shared with anyone. A scary prospect, eh? Well, so it was that day. As the trainer asked us to do this, he made it clear that we didn't have to take part. From memory, perhaps one-third of the room immediately took him up on the offer. He asked those still involved to write our answer, fold the paper up as tightly as possible and then hand it to him. At that point, another third decided it wasn't for them. The thought of handing it over to a relative stranger was too much. But there were still some people willing to follow through, which meant the trainer revealed the next step: we were to come up one by one, pick a piece of paper, read it out and then ask whose piece of paper that was. As you can probably imagine, this was the moment of truth for those of us left, and almost everybody still in the mix then decided not to take it further. Of course, the trainer then revealed that he wouldn't be doing anything of the sort, so we could all relax and keep our pieces of paper. He used this exercise to demonstrate how difficult it is for people to share their private thoughts by making us would-be counsellors step into the shoes of our future clients and really feel and experience what they would be going through. It was a brilliant way of showing how much respect you should have for people willing to break their silence. It's also a powerful way for me to remind you that sharing is hard for anyone, which is why the first stage of noticing is critical. It's non-judgemental, non-threatening and not asking anything of anyone at that stage.

So, there's a critical difference between noticing and interpreting when understanding and supporting other people and their mental health. In the journey towards a kinder, more compassionate and mentally healthy workplace, noticing is a powerful way to make an enormous difference. Next time you come across someone who seems to be doing any of the things we opened this chapter with, please remember the value of noticing and offer your understanding, empathy and support without judgement. You might change someone's life for the better or, in some cases, even save it.

It is time to notice, not interpret, to help others break their silence.

'In the midst of winter, I found there was,
within me, an invincible summer.'

Albert Camus

Chapter 14
Inspiring others by sharing vulnerability

There is a quote from Brené Brown, a renowned researcher and author, that beautifully encapsulates why sharing vulnerability and being vulnerable is so powerful. 'Sharing our vulnerability can inspire others to embrace their authenticity and take bold steps toward growth and transformation.'

In the early days of my career, it was rare to find leaders and managers willing to share their vulnerabilities openly. Leadership was seen as the domain of those who were certain, strong and invulnerable. I've learned through my work, though, that when leaders show vulnerability, it creates the trust, openness and flexibility of thought which create the conditions that inspire the innovation, creativity and change Brown describes. It can help build stronger relationships within and across teams and between teams and their leaders.

There is now a noticeable shift towards a more compassionate and authentic leadership style, which is good, but we still need to go much further. I know this because I've witnessed some extraordinary examples of the difference it has made when senior leaders share their vulnerabilities.

I remember a particular incident during a session at a well-known law firm several years ago. As I spoke, I noticed everyone suddenly diverting their attention elsewhere. Eventually, I spotted a tall man, the senior partner of the firm, standing up. At that moment, he revealed the real reason for inviting me to talk about creating kinder cultures. He was in therapy. This very successful lawyer, clearly perceived as an alpha male, openly admitted that he had been struggling mentally and needed help. At that moment, you could have heard a pin drop. People were taken aback by what he said. He went as far as showing his medication to prove his point. He wanted to share that it had been a challenging year for him and that he was seeking support.

It was a courageous moment that inspired others to follow suit.

Soon after, during the session, three or four other senior individuals also confessed their mental health struggles, each person wanting to share their own stories for the first time. They discovered that sharing their stories didn't make them appear weak or a liability to the organisation. On the contrary, they became an inspiration to others. One woman even confessed that she had not told the full truth on her CV. She had taken off her bachelor's degree in mental health, fearing it would hinder her chances of working for this firm. Seeing the CEO's vulnerability and his honesty gave her the courage to tell the truth.

My experience extends to working with the military at a senior level. You might well assume it would be challenging to get high-ranking individuals in the military to discuss how they feel openly but I witnessed another extraordinary moment during my time with them. A senior military figure decided to speak about the mental breakdown he had experienced in his career, which he never thought he would, or could, talk about. He described the fact that, throughout his breakdown, the silence was deafening. Not one person talked about it. He managed to bounce back and achieve even greater success in his career, but that breakdown clearly greatly impacted him. Tears streamed down his face as he shared his story and others in the room, mostly men, were also moved to tears. Once he finished, others immediately wanted to share their own stories. Sharing struggles and vulnerabilities with others can have a profound impact on them. I was amazed when I opened up about my vulnerabilities and discovered that friends whom I had known for 20 or 30 years had gone through similar experiences. They wished I had confided in them earlier so we could all have supported each other. It's remarkable how many individuals never break their silence, even within their closest circles, until someone takes the first step to share.

Despite these stories, I know the workplace is still generally considered a space for professionalism and composure, where vulnerability is often seen as a sign of weakness. However, the reality is that sharing vulnerability at work can be a powerful tool for leadership, inspiration, and team building. Based on my experience, let me share why I believe that sharing vulnerability at work is essential and how it can inspire others while fostering a more positive, productive and, ultimately, kinder culture.

Authentic leadership is about being true to yourself and transparent with others. When leaders are open about their vulnerabilities, it humanises them and makes them relatable to their teams. Authentic leaders are more likely to gain the trust and respect of their employees because they are perceived as genuine and trustworthy. Think about a time when you had a boss who openly acknowledged their struggles or admitted when they made a mistake. Chances are, you felt a stronger connection to that leader because you saw them as someone who understood your challenges and uncertainties.

We all know that trust is the foundation of any healthy working relationship. When leaders share their vulnerabilities, it creates an atmosphere of trust and psychological safety within the team. Team members feel more comfortable sharing their concerns, ideas and challenges when they see their leader doing the same. Imagine working in an environment where you can openly discuss your difficulties without fear of judgement or reprisal. This environment fosters cooperation, ingenuity and imagination, as team members are more likely to contribute their unique perspectives and ideas.

Sharing vulnerability can also inspire personal and professional growth. When leaders openly discuss their areas of improvement or the obstacles they have overcome, it encourages employees to view challenges as opportunities for growth rather than setbacks. We know from a previous chapter how important that is. For example, a manager who shares their journey of overcoming a career setback can motivate employees to persevere through challenges. This inspiration can lead to increased resilience and a willingness to take calculated risks.

Remember how important empathy is in our ability to understand the feelings of others. When leaders share their vulnerabilities, they demonstrate empathy toward their team members. This empathy, in turn, encourages a culture of compassion and support. Consider a leader who openly acknowledges the stress and anxiety of a major project deadline. This acknowledgement can prompt team members to offer support, share strategies for managing stress or provide a listening ear. In this way, vulnerability becomes a catalyst for further empathy and connection.

Of course, it's one thing to understand why sharing vulnerability at work is essential, but how to do it effectively is another skill altogether, so I thought it would be worth ending this chapter with a few examples of ways in which I've seen others do it well. Not every moment is suitable for sharing vulnerability at work. It's essential to choose the right time and place to do so. For example, during a team meeting or one-on-one check-in, you may find a natural opportunity to discuss a personal challenge or share an experience that taught you a valuable lesson. Authenticity is critical when sharing vulnerability. Be honest about your experiences, emotions and thoughts. Authenticity breeds trust and trust is the foundation of any meaningful connection.

One effective way to share vulnerability is through personal stories. These stories can be related to your career journey, challenges you've overcome or moments of self-doubt that led to growth. Sharing personal stories helps others relate to your experiences and see that vulnerability is a part of the human experience. When sharing vulnerability, normalise imperfection.

Emphasise that mistakes, encountering obstacles and facing difficulties is ok. This reassurance can alleviate team members' pressure to perform perfectly. Sharing vulnerability should not be a one-way street. Encourage open dialogue so that team members feel comfortable sharing their vulnerabilities and experiences. This dialogue creates a culture of mutual support and understanding. Finally, when sharing vulnerability, emphasise the positive takeaways and lessons learned. Highlight how your vulnerabilities have contributed to your personal and professional growth. This process helps inspire hope and optimism in others, even in the face of challenges.

Sharing vulnerability at work is not a sign of weakness but of strength. It fosters trust, empathy and connection within teams, leading to a more positive and productive work environment. As leaders, it's vital to lead by example, demonstrating that vulnerability can be a powerful tool for inspiration and growth. Doing so can create workplaces where individuals feel valued, supported and inspired to reach their full potential. It's also a powerful reminder to everyone around you that we all share many of the same vulnerabilities.

I want to finish this chapter with a final story that perfectly illustrates the power of sharing vulnerability. As part of my involvement in a graduate selection process some years ago, I was on the team tasked with assessing candidates presenting something they felt passionately about. It was in front of a large audience and the standards proved to be exceptionally high. I'll always remember when Abigail took the floor and revealed her topic. She wanted to talk about her bipolar disorder. The reaction from the room was incredible. You could have heard a pin drop. Her honesty and courage made her presentation impossible to forget. When it came to decision time, Abigail's name was at the top of everyone's list of graduates to hire. Her star had shone very brightly in one of the most competitive recruitment landscapes. In sharing her vulnerability, she inspired everyone that day. Sometimes, we could all do with being a bit more like Abigail.

It is time to break the silence.

'It's hard to be a friend to someone who is depressed,
but it is one of the kindest,
noblest and best things you will ever do.'

Stephen Fry

Chapter 15
Put your oxygen mask on first

Ladies and gentlemen, in the unlikely event of a sudden loss of cabin pressure, oxygen masks will drop down from the overhead compartments. With your seatbelt fastened, please remain seated and pull the mask down to start the oxygen flow. Cover your nose and mouth and breathe normally. Please ensure you put your mask on before assisting children or other passengers. Make sure your mask is secure before helping others. Thank you for choosing Beeney's Budget Airline and we hope you have a pleasant flight.

I'm not sure I'd really like the thought of Beeney's Budget Airline, but I love this metaphor for how we should approach our lives and prioritise our wellbeing. Ultimately, on a plane, putting your mask on first before assisting others is crucial because if you don't have a steady supply of oxygen, you won't be able to function, making it difficult or impossible to help others. It's the same when we think about our approach to wellbeing. If you don't look after yourself, you'll find it impossible to look after others and this is the focus of this chapter. How do you put your oxygen mask on first, and, importantly, what does that oxygen mask look like for organisations? But first, as you've come to expect by now, a story that powerfully illustrates my point from my own experience.

Six years ago, the managing director of one of my clients, who oversaw a region within a large engineering company, contacted me privately. He wanted to meet one-on-one and told me his company would cover the cost. Naturally I agreed, curious and concerned about what might be wrong. On the day, he told me that he generally had an easy time in life. He was a managing director in his 30s and his career was progressing exceptionally well. He told me that he was best known at work as someone who was unflappable. Despite all of that, he felt a failure.

'I'm failing at something for the first time, David, and I can't handle it.'

I can still hear the emotion in his voice that day, even now. I asked him what he was struggling with. He confided in me and told me that he thought he was failing at being a dad.

'I feel like I'm just not cut out for it. I'm rubbish at it.'

As I got to know him better, I learned that he had become a father about a year earlier but due to his demanding career and the long hours he worked, he decided he needed to create more time for his wife and child. He gave up three significant parts of his life: running, his West Ham season ticket and attending car rallies. Many people might naturally applaud him for these sacrifices. Still, as I got to know him better, it became clear that he had developed a form of postnatal depression because he had forgotten to put his oxygen mask on first.

We worked together to reintroduce those things he had given up. He started running again, enjoyed watching West Ham play and attended his beloved car rallies. Six years have passed since that pivotal moment and he now has three children. He believes he's a great dad which, of course, he always was. He just didn't think it at the time. He still finds time to go to West Ham matches, runs regularly and follows his passion for those car rallies. His career has become even busier, but he has learned to appreciate the importance of looking after himself. When he first became a dad, his instinct was to focus entirely on others which was a mistake because, by losing the things he loved, his happiness declined and the depression he suffered meant he couldn't engage fully with the wife and child for whom he had sacrificed the activities he enjoyed. Giving up the things that took his time sounded like a logical solution, but it just led to him not being able to help and support his family. He had to put his oxygen mask back on. I'm also aware, of course, of the importance of mums putting their oxygen masks on first too and how hard it often is for them because society still casts women as caregivers first and foremost. In truth, that's a topic for an entire library of books, but I didn't want to end the story without acknowledging that.

Looking after yourself first really matters; it's not selfish and here's why. Life isn't easy, as we know. But if you put that mask on first, it's like hitting the reset button for your mind. When you look after yourself, you feel good about yourself. And in doing that, you send a powerful message to yourself that you are worth caring about. This way of boosting your self-esteem can help protect your mental health when life's challenges are thrown your way. Setting healthy boundaries is a critical part of putting yourself first. It's about saying no when you need to and prioritising your wellbeing. This process reduces stress and protects your mental health from being overwhelmed by the demands of others. The more you look after yourself, the more mental clarity and energy you build to tackle tasks and think creatively. It's also clear from all my work that the more you care for your mental wellbeing, the better you can communicate, empathise and connect with those around you.

That helps frame why putting your oxygen mask on first is critical, but I'm often asked how to do this and what that looks like. My answer and advice are always the same and, although I don't talk about it as seven steps, it is precisely that: the seven steps towards giving yourself the best chance of prioritising your wellbeing. So, here they are, all common sense and obvious, but the point is to intentionally focus on them. This list can act as a guide for you. It can also be something you look back on frequently as a reminder of what you need to be intentional about. Remember the phrase we've used already in this book; that which you pay attention to grows, so it's time to pay attention!

Three of the seven are so well documented that you don't need me to add much. These three are sleep, diet and physical exercise. Sleep is not just about feeling rested; it's like a mental reset button. When you sleep well, your brain processes emotions, sharpens focus and keeps stress in check. It's the foundation of good mental health. It's also true that eating isn't just about your waistline; it also affects your brain. Nutrient-rich foods like fruits, vegetables and lean protein provide the fuel your brain and body need to function at its best. And finally, physical exercise. It's not just for the body; it's a brain booster. When you get moving, your brain releases feel-good chemicals like endorphins, which can reduce anxiety and depression. Plus, it improves blood flow to the brain, helping with cognitive function and memory. The best part? These three amigos aren't just solo acts but a dynamic trio that work together. Regular exercise can improve sleep and a balanced diet can enhance your workout performance. When you prioritise sleep, eat well and stay active, you're setting yourself up for a happier and healthier mind.

Next up from our seven steps are two things that run around in the same gang but are different. We've already talked about one of them in this book: playtime. Playtime's mental health friend is me-time, which is all about self-care and rejuvenation and that's been the focus of this chapter. It's those moments when you carve out space to relax, recharge, and do things that make you feel good. Whether reading a book, watching that favourite box set series or simply meditating in quiet solitude, me-time is like hitting the pause button in a busy life. It allows you to reflect, destress and regain mental clarity. It's essential because it helps prevent burnout and keeps you in tune with your needs. On the flip side, as we've already described in the book, playtime is like a mental playground. It's when you engage in activities purely for enjoyment and fun. Think about hobbies, sports or any creative outlet that brings joy to your heart. It encourages creativity, boosts mood and fosters a sense of accomplishment. Playtime and fun are not just for kids; adults need them too, remember! Playing is a break from the routine, reminding you that life isn't just about responsibilities but also about experiencing joy and spontaneity.

The sixth step is an important one: having something to look forward to. Having that in our lives injects a dose of positivity. It creates a sense of anticipation, excitement and purpose, which can counteract feelings of stagnation and depression. Knowing enjoyable events are on the horizon can boost our overall mental wellbeing, provide motivation and give us a much brighter outlook on life. I will turn to a good friend for the seventh and final step. 'Beeney,' this friend will often say to me, 'There are two types of people in the world. The ones who, when you meet them, energise you, motivate you, make you laugh and who you can't wait to see again. They're life's radiators and you must hang out with them.' He will then continue, 'On the other hand, you know those people who turn up and, even before they've opened their mouths, you feel worse about yourself because of their negative energy? They're the drains. You must avoid them like a handshake during the flu season.'

There are those in the world who can be entire central heating systems. The warmth of their energy and zest for life is infectious and hugely positive. On the other hand, we all know what an entire sewage works smells like and being around a sewage works can make your life stink. Surround yourself with people who energise and lift you up; they should be your tribe.

It is the responsibility of all organisations to help employees with their oxygen masks. They do this by consistently demonstrating that their people are the lifeblood of the organisation. When individuals feel supported, healthy and motivated, they perform at their best. It means that the part of their life that is work is both rewarding and enjoyable. This, in turn, leads to increased productivity, innovation and employee retention, all directly impacting an organisation's bottom line. We now know this to be true beyond any reasonable doubt. When companies prioritise the wellbeing of their employees, they create a positive work culture that attracts top talent and fosters loyalty. Employees who feel valued and supported are likelier to go the extra mile, improving customer satisfaction and enhancing brand reputation. And, in today's competitive business world, where talent and innovation are crucial differentiators, organisations that understand the importance of putting their oxygen mask on first by investing in their people are better positioned to adapt, grow and succeed in the face of the many challenges they face.

It is time to break the silence by putting your oxygen mask on first.

'Never apologise for how you feel.
No one can control how they feel.
The sun doesn't apologise for being the sun.
The rain doesn't say sorry for falling. Feelings just are.'

Idris Elba

Chapter 16
The proof of the pudding

The American essayist and philosopher, Ralph Waldon Emerson once said, 'Life is a journey, not a destination.' You find it on countless Pinterest boards and Instagram posts. That's because it resonates and speaks to one of life's great truisms. The journey we are all on consists of many things of which two of the most important are your learned and your lived experience. In this book, you've been given a window through which you've been able to read about both my learned and lived experience in the hope that this helps your life's journey. The learned experience I've had through my work and the many people who have supported me along the way. And my lived experience through my personal struggles and their impact on my life's journey. But there's one last lived experience that I want to share with you before you close the pages of this book. It's an experience that demonstrates that there is proof in the pudding of my advice. I have practised what I preach and I know it works.

Between 2003 and 2008, I had the privilege of serving as the general manager of Auto Trader in North London. This job was an opportunity I couldn't refuse because it allowed me to shape a business according to my vision. My goal was to foster a culture that would drive significant commercial success. When I took over, our region was considered the worst-performing in the UK. However, within three years, we had become one of the best performing. This turnaround is one of my proudest achievements as a leader. That we were able to sustain the top position in the company league tables for year-on-year growth until the magazine division's closure in 2009 is a testament to the effectiveness of the advice I share in this book, much of which is based on what I did in that role. I recount this story not to boast or to ask for a pat on the back, but to illustrate the power of kindness, employee engagement and prioritising wellbeing in the workplace. That success is the proof of what a kinder culture leads to. It's important to say here that this success was not down to me alone. I had the great fortune of having a brilliant leader in my managing director, Sharon Randall, who gave me the freedom to operate and to whom I've referred a lot throughout this book. I also had the joy of having Ranjit (Tony) Doal, as my right-hand man. Ranjit was exceptional at motivating and inspiring people and, again, I learned so much from working with him. It was a privilege to be in a team with such talented people.

Our collective commitment to cultivating a kind and vibrant workplace culture was central to our success. We didn't view fun as a mere frivolity but as a crucial part of our ethos. We introduced initiatives like regular awards nights, fancy dress theme days and offsite strategy days. Believe it or not, I even performed the David Brent dance for charity in the middle of our accounts department. These initiatives created an environment where employees felt valued, engaged and motivated. They also promoted structured time for unstructured conversations, a concept you'll recall as being vital and one that Sharon was completely committed to. It's a principle I've continued to value both as a leader and now as an educator and campaigner. As a leader, I used humour to unlock creativity and productivity and to bring people together. Despite its proven ability to foster an environment where people can bring their best, this approach is still underutilised by leaders today. Remember that adults need playtime too.

A significant factor in our success was our focus on people development. Unlike other regions, we invested substantially in training and development, bringing in top-notch trainers who profoundly impacted our skills and competencies. As senior leaders, we set the tone by prioritising employee wellbeing. Our managers made a concerted effort to know their team members on a personal level. I always kept the story of Sally's dog in mind whenever I had new people on my team. This investment in our people yielded enormous dividends. We enjoyed a low staff turnover rate and high levels of employee satisfaction. Sales meetings were never just about business; they were opportunities for genuine connections among team members.

Starting meetings with personal check-ins and discussions helped foster camaraderie and trust, laying the foundation for effective collaboration and teamwork. This emphasis on building relationships beyond the workplace contributed to a powerful sense of belonging and loyalty.

I remember how infectious the passion and dedication of our team was. It created a positive ripple effect that extended through to our customers. Employees' genuine enthusiasm for the business undoubtedly contributed to the region's loyal customer following and sustained growth. This alignment of employee passion with organisational goals created a virtuous cycle of success, where satisfied customers further fuelled our teams' motivation and commitment. Looking back at this period in my career gives me a massive sense of pride. We built a successful business, which allowed me to embark on a personal journey of self-discovery and learning.

Carl Rogers was an American psychologist whose work I have long admired. Known for his person-centred approach to therapy, he recognised the importance of creating certain core conditions for individuals to flourish. The culture we created exemplified many of these core conditions, including empathy, honesty, kindness and unconditional support. It yielded excellent business success but, more importantly, allowed our people to flourish. Carl Rogers believes people can achieve incredible things with the right environment and support. 'When I look at the world, I'm pessimistic, but when I look at people, I'm optimistic,' he once said. I could not agree more.

It's amazing what you can achieve when you help people break their silence.

'When the world comes crashing at your feet, it's okay
to let others help pick up the pieces.
If we're present to take part in your happiness when
your circumstances are great, we are more than capable
of sharing your pain.'

'The Sun and Her Flowers'
from Rupi Kaur

Chapter 17
The clock is ticking

Mental health in the workplace has for too long been relegated to the shadows. It's been a hidden battle fought silently behind closed doors and masked by the carefully curated façade of professionalism. We can no longer ignore it. It must be brought into the light for the sake of every person and every organisation and to create the kinder cultures we so desperately need.

We all must break the silence because silence creates an extraordinarily heavy burden. It's a weight that grows heavier with each passing day, each suppressed emotion and each unspoken truth. In the workplace, the silence surrounding mental health is the most dangerous one of all with real and devastating consequences.

You only need to look at the numbers to see this. According to the World Health Organization, depression and anxiety cost the global economy over $1 trillion each year in lost productivity. It's not just about the economic impact. It's also about the human cost—the cost of individuals suffering in silence, afraid to admit they need help. It's about the missed opportunities for support, understanding and connection that can make a difference.

We know that silence breeds stigma. It perpetuates the myth that mental health challenges are a sign of weakness, that they should be hidden and not spoken about, and that seeking help is a mark of failure. But, despite all that, there is hope. The dawn of a new era in understanding mental health at work is upon us and we are at a turning point: a moment when we must collectively decide to break the silence and take meaningful action. The pandemic forced the world to confront the importance of mental health in a way like never before. The isolation, uncertainty and loss that many experienced during the pandemic have underscored the critical need for mental health support in all aspects of life, including the workplace. While many organisations are still in the dark ages with regards to mental health, forward-thinking ones now recognise that their most valuable asset is their people and that kindness wins. They understand that employees are not robots but complex human beings with emotional needs. These companies are investing in mental health programmes like mine and creating a culture of empathy and understanding. I now meet individuals every week who are finding their voices and sharing their stories. They are breaking the silence by opening up about their struggles with mental health at work. These stories humanise the issue, showing that it can happen to any one of us and that seeking help is ok.

Breaking the silence on mental health at work is not just a nice idea; it's an urgent necessity. It's a call to action that requires a global commitment and effort. We must begin by acknowledging that it's ok not to be ok. We need to recognise the signs of mental distress in ourselves and our colleagues and offer support without judgement. Seeking help should be seen as an act of courage, not weakness. Companies must take the lead in creating mentally healthy workplaces. This means investing in mental health programmes, training managers to recognise and support employees in need and fostering a culture of openness and acceptance. Finally, let's use education as it is best used: as a powerful tool for change. Employees should be educated about mental health, including the signs of common conditions like depression and anxiety.

Imagine that workplace I painted at the beginning of this book - one where employees can openly discuss their mental health without fear of judgement. One where seeking help for mental health challenges is as normal as seeking treatment for a physical illness. One where every organisation prioritises the wellbeing of its employees and recognises that a mentally healthy workforce is productive, innovative and resilient.

This brighter tomorrow is within our reach, but we all must break the silence. It demands colossal courage, empathy and a collective commitment to change. It starts with you, me and everyone who refuses to let silence be the status quo. Of course, the journey to a universally mentally healthy workplace is not without its challenges, but the potential rewards are immense. It's a journey that will not only save lives but also enhance the quality of those lives. It's also a journey that will make our workplaces more productive, our employees more engaged and our society more compassionate.

As for that clock, it is now ticking. Will you join us on this critical journey? Will you be the voice of change, the advocate for those who cannot speak and the catalyst for a brighter, more compassionate future in which kinder cultures exist everywhere? The choice is yours.

The positive impact of breaking the silence is immeasurable.

'I am not afraid of storms, for
I am learning how to sail my ship.'

Louisa May Alcott,
Little Women

A final thought

The ghost-writer is rarely given their voice in a book. I must admit that I wasn't keen to break that mould. But after some gentle badgering from David, I was persuaded that it might be the right way to close a book that has been a memorable journey for me.

I didn't know David well before we embarked on this project. One of my closest friends, Suki Thompson, introduced me to him. It's with a broken heart that I use the past tense because Suki passed away on 30 July 2023. She was a remarkable woman and I miss her very much, but her spirit and memory live on. This book is just one of the many ways that is true. Without Suki, it may never have happened. Her ability to connect people in incredibly meaningful ways was extraordinary.

How lucky I was that Suki introduced me to David. Hopefully you'll have understood his extraordinary passion for making a difference by now. Some people who have read this book will know David well; others will have encountered him through his work. But for those who don't know the David Beeney I've come to know and love, let me say this.

He is one in a million. Kind to a fault, profoundly human and someone with the incredible ability to engage a room. He believes passionately in the importance of creating kinder cultures. He has made it his life's work to ensure more people can speak out more often about their feelings. In doing so, he is taking on one of the most critical challenges of our age. I can think of no finer individual to be leading that cause. He deserves all our support and as much advocacy as we can all muster. It's why I wanted to help him write his book and why we must rally around his purpose.

Writing this book with David has been one of the most profoundly important things I've done in my career. In my experience, the relationship between the ghost-writer and their subject is unlike anything I've encountered professionally. It can become your obsession, teacher and creative outlet in equal measure. It is sometimes frustrating and exhausting, but the rewards are always extraordinary.

Understanding the power of vulnerability through this book has allowed me to share my fears and experiences more openly with the people who matter most to me. In doing so, I am beginning to discover that vulnerability is not a weakness but a tower of strength. It's the bridge that connects us all and the common thread that binds us in our shared humanity.

One of the most profound lessons I've also learned is that the human experience is incredibly complex. Mental health is not a monolithic entity; it's a deeply intricate web of thoughts, emotions and experiences. There are no easy answers or one-size-fits-all solutions; a book like this can only open doors for people. Each person's journey with mental health is unique but we can all do more to support each other, look after each other and look out for each other.

Everyone has their own story and everyone's story truly matters. If we can all acknowledge that and spend more time valuing the power of listening to each other, the world will be a much better place. Nowhere is this better articulated than in the power of the question, 'how are you?' It can be one of the most meaningless questions we often ask each other, but in the hands of people who understand its true power, it's a question that can save lives.

We should always appreciate the ripple effect of empathy. One of this book's golden threads is that we all have an important role in helping break the silence. Our own, our families, our work colleagues and perhaps even strangers we meet by chance. Sparking conversations about mental health in whatever place and encouraging people to extend the hand of human kindness is not a box-ticking exercise. It's a fundamental part of why we are alive. While writing this book, my son suffered a torrid time with his mental health as a professional cricketer. Because of that, I witnessed the devastating impact of too many leaders with neither the head nor the heart to grasp even the most basic principles in this book. As I've reflected on my career while writing this book, I know there are times when I have also been one of those leaders. Some of the ways I chose to lead at specific points in my career demanded more empathy and sensitivity than I showed. I was a young man in too much of a hurry and would have benefitted beyond measure from a coach like David. It was a different time, but it was made so much worse for not embracing all the guiding principles in this book.

In my son's case, thanks to some wonderful friends and his family, he has emerged happier, healthier and with a much greater sense of purpose. I also watched with pride and admiration as he broke his silence about what he was going through. In doing so, I know he has already helped others to break theirs. His was a single voice with a single story and a reminder that our actions, no matter how small, can create a more compassionate and understanding world.

I am a lifelong learner and the longer I live, the more I realise that I am always far from being the smartest person in the room. Our understanding of our mental health and the human mind is continually expanding and our workplaces are now in constant flux. I hope this book gives people food for thought as we navigate these issues and this new world. I also hope it highlights that there is always more to discover and understand and that we should all approach this issue with curiosity and an open heart.

When we embarked on this book, I told David that we would have succeeded if what we wrote encouraged just one person to break their silence. As the Chinese proverb tells us, a journey of 1000 miles begins with a single step. 'Breaking the Silence' has been more than a book for me. It's been the most incredible reminder that we are all part of a much larger tapestry woven together by our shared humanity and the ups and downs that define a life. We should all travel towards a place where mental health is not stigmatised but embraced for what it is. Something that impacts one in one of us and needs all of us to recognise that in life, kindness wins and that we all must have each other's backs. Here's to a world where we all continue to break the silence, one heartfelt conversation at a time.

Thank you, David, for all you do and for allowing me to share your extraordinary story.

It truly is time to break the silence.

Thank you

From a standing start in October 2016 to being listed two years later as one of the top global influencers in employee engagement. That success would never have happened without the support of some incredible people around me over many years and the odd slice of luck. As it turned out, I had several strokes of good fortune within my first few months. That's more than most people's fair share and there are many to thank for that.

Firstly, Paul Gibson, whose unexpected challenge propelled me into uncharted territory. Sixteen days into my new business, I presented to a significant group of HR specialists at an event in Cambridge. Without Paul pushing me to do so, it would never have happened. That belief in my abilities lit the way for my business. I will be forever grateful to Paul and the event's chairperson, Richard DeNetto.

My lifelong friend, Steve Baker, played a pivotal role by facilitating an early and crucial introduction to Emmajane Varley and Birgit Neu of HSBC. Steve's initiative set the stage for some fantastic opportunities for me, including delivering a global webinar for all HSBC managers. Thank you, Steve, for your unwavering support and friendship.

I'm indebted to the wonderful Micky Denehy and Gail Clark for opening doors and championing me, leading to an early collaboration with Sainsbury's. Their support was instrumental in shaping the trajectory of Breaking The Silence in those very early months.

I'm so grateful to Jane Austin for providing an early platform to showcase my work. Budget constraints then meant a long bus ride to Durham, but her support ignited a fantastic partnership with Wave Utilities that continues today.

A special mention must go to Matt Manners, from Inspiring Workplaces, and Ruth Dance for their enduring drive to bolster my global credibility. Their recognition has been so invaluable.

I also owe sincere thanks to Keith Knowles for recognising the potential of my work and providing opportunities and introductions, particularly in supporting the mental health initiatives of the Royal Navy.

Sharon, Nigel and Grace Slattery are a family forever etched in my heart. Their unwavering support during the early stages of my business was a lifeline, whilst their extraordinary generosity and encouragement went beyond what even the closest of friendships might reasonably have offered.

I'm also immensely grateful to Tracy Wilkinson, Anne-Marie Russell, Rachel Meakins and Jess Hannan for their advocacy and collaboration which have been instrumental in expanding the reach of my work.

A very special thank you goes to Garry Lace. His drive, energy and gift with words have been the engine room of this entire project. His and his team's mission at Storians is to help tell better stories and they have done that beyond measure for me. I never dreamed I would publish a book in my lifetime but here it is and I couldn't be prouder.

Behind every great person (or even very average in my case) is someone even more remarkable. I first met Lisa Toone at the end of March 2017 when I was struggling to monetise my work. It is no coincidence that, as our relationship grew, so did my business. I would not have succeeded without Lisa's unconditional love and support over the last seven years. We married in July 2021 and Lisa is now known affectionately by me as Mrs Beans.

Finally, Lisa and I would also like to acknowledge the love of our family and thank our exceptional children, Joel, Jodie, and Casey, for making us proud every day, along with our grandchildren Riley, Noah and Brody. Brody is no longer with us but remains a profound part of us and our family. My mum, who recently passed away, would be so chuffed that I have written this book. She would be even prouder that my commitment to help more people break their silence is stronger than ever. It's a life's work but I couldn't be more grateful that it is my life's work. Let's get going on the journey together.

It's now time for you to help break the silence.

Here's what 'Breaking the Silence' has told you.

These are the ways to build your emotional resilience and take better care of yourself and others.

You treasure what you measure. Find a way to check in with your mental health and take it more seriously.

We all face moments of vulnerability and hardship. Accept it's ok not to be ok and be gentle and kind with yourself.

Self-care is not selfish. If you don't look after yourself, you'll find it impossible to look after others.

Employing a growth mindset will lead to greater optimism, an improved sense of self and a willingness to ask for help.

Celebrate what you have rather than what you don't have. That way, you'll discover the real value of gratitude.

Sharing your vulnerability will inspire others. It is no longer seen as a sign of weakness but as a tower of strength.

Slowing down allows us to foster deeper connections and be more present and attentive in the moments that matter.

Engaging in playful activities stimulates our imagination. It also triggers the release of endorphins and is a powerful stress reliever.

Making time for leisure pursuits and spending time with loved ones helps you to maintain a healthy work-life balance. It will also help you find more resilience through your workplace challenges.

Have a strategy for recognising a change in your wellbeing. Consider keeping a sleep diary and track your energy and enjoyment levels.

Self-compassion can boost your resilience and help you be less self-critical. It will also create a healthier work environment and help you achieve more.

Delegating is a critical skill for personal and professional growth. It's not about being lazy or incapable; it's about being intelligent and strategic.

Set realistic, sensible goals and pat yourself on the back for both the little wins and the big ones.

Micro-sprints help avoid burnout and mental fatigue while accomplishing more in less time.

Sleep is not just about feeling rested; it's like a mental reset button. When you sleep well, your brain processes emotions, sharpens focus and keeps stress in check. It's the foundation of good mental health.

A healthy diet is a healthy mind: what you eat and drink affects your brain. Nutrient-rich foods like fruits, vegetables and lean proteins provide the fuel your brain needs to function at its best. When you eat well, you will generally feel better about yourself.

Physical exercise is not just for the body; it's a brain booster. When you get moving your brain releases feel-good chemicals like endorphins, which can reduce anxiety and depression. It also improves blood flow to the brain, helping with cognitive function and memory.

The dynamic trio of sleep, exercise, and diet work superbly together. Regular exercise can improve sleep and a balanced diet can enhance your workout performance. When you prioritise sleep, eat well and stay active, you're setting yourself up for a happier and healthier mind.

'Me time' is like hitting the pause button in a busy life. It allows you to reflect, de-stress and regain mental clarity. It's essential because it helps prevent burnout and keeps you in tune with your needs.

We all need things to look forward to. They create a sense of anticipation, excitement and purpose, all of which provide motivation and give us a much brighter outlook on life.

Surround yourself with people who love and respect you and make you feel good about yourself. The more time you spend with people chipping away at your self-confidence, the more damage they are doing to your mental health.

These are the ways to create kinder cultures and for leaders to nurture their teams.

We understand the language of one to 10, so let's use it to check in with our teams and keep an eye out for change.

To develop and maintain a culture of kindness, it must start at the very top. A fish rots from its head.

Ensure all line managers understand their immense responsibility to nurture, support and care for the people on their team.

Prioritise helping others, knowing you never arrive as a leader and can always learn more. Every day is a school day.

Harness the power of asking, 'How are you?' Ask it twice and you will be amazed at the impact it has.

When you initiate non-work conversations, amazing things happen. You boost morale and cultivate a supportive atmosphere where individuals feel valued beyond their professional contributions.

Acknowledging each other's personal lives makes individuals feel understood and supported, which increases resilience and improves productivity.

Mindful listening helps create an environment where people can be seen, appreciated and valued for who they are.

Playtime in the workplace is a commercial imperative. The balance between work and play is crucial for employee wellbeing and productivity.

Communication matters. Leaders who value it will engage in more open and honest conversations about mental health issues.

Leaders who are prepared to open the 'can of worms' surrounding the stigma of mental health foster a happier, healthier and more productive workforce.

Lowering expectations never equates to lowering standards or compromising excellence. Instead, it involves setting realistic and meaningful goals whilst being mindful of people's needs and circumstances.

When we notice rather than interpret, we create a kind, compassionate and understanding environment where people feel safe sharing their experiences.

Leaders who show genuine vulnerability can inspire innovation, creativity and change. They can also help build stronger relationships and trust among teams.

Authentic leaders are more likely to gain the trust and respect of their employees because they are perceived as genuine and trustworthy.

In workplaces, you must be able to discuss your difficulties without fear of judgement or reprisal. That type of environment fosters cooperation, ingenuity and imagination where team members are more likely to contribute their unique perspectives and ideas.

Demonstrating empathy towards team members encourages a culture of compassion and support.

Sharing vulnerability at work is not a sign of weakness. It is a sign of strength and authenticity and builds trust and empathy. This results in a more positive and productive work environment.

When companies prioritise the wellbeing of their employees, they create a work culture that attracts top talent and fosters loyalty. Employees who feel valued and supported are more likely to go the extra mile, improving customer satisfaction and enhancing brand reputation.

Make fun a crucial part of your company ethos.

Promote and create structured time for unstructured conversations.

Investing in mental health programmes and training managers to recognise and support employees who need it most will foster a culture of openness and drive employee energy.

The journey to a world where we remove the stigma of mental health will make our workplaces more productive, our employees more engaged and our society more compassionate.

Notes and further reading

Adam Morgan and Mark Barden, A Beautiful Constraint: How to Transform Your Limitations into Advantages, and Why It's Everyone's Business.

Héctor García and Francesc Miralles, Ikigai. The Japanese Secret to a Long and Happy Life.

Carol Dweck, Mindset. Changing the Way You Think to Fulfil Your Potential Elizabeth Dunn and Michael Norton, Happy Money: The New Science of Smarter Spending.

Austin Suellentrop and E. Beth Bauman, How Influential Is a Good Manager? https://www.gallup.com/cliftonstrengths/en/350423/influential-good-manager.aspx.

Stuart Brown M.D. and Christopher Vaughan, Play: How It Shapes the Brain, Opens the Imagination, and Invigorates the Soul.

Cassie Mogilner and the Knowledge at Wharton staff, Does Variety Fuel Happiness at Work and in Life? It Depends. https://knowledge.wharton.upenn.edu/article/does-variety-fuel-happiness-at-work-and-in-life-it-depends.

Deloitte, Mental Health and Employers. The case for investment - pandemic and beyond, March 2022.

Kristin Neff, Self-Compassion: The Proven Power of Being Kind to Yourself.

For further reading on the power of vulnerability, try Brené Brown, Daring Greatly.

For further reading on person-centred therapy, try Carl Rogers, On Becoming a Person: A Therapist's View of Psychotherapy.